MISSION
DRIVEN

MISSION DRIVEN

CelebrityPress®
Lake Mary, Florida

CONTENTS

CHAPTER 1

SOMEBODY OUGHT TO DO SOMETHING

BY KENI THOMAS

The radio exploded in a high-pitched oration as someone frantically reported,

"We have a Black Hawk going down….There's a Black Hawk going down…We've got a Black Hawk crashed in the city!"

…and just like that, everything changed.

The original mission had been a daring daylight raid into the city of Mogadishu in order to apprehend two high-valued targets on our most-wanted list. The HVTs were holding a secret meeting at a building located smack dab in the middle of the Bakaara market, a known enemy stronghold. If we could launch and get there within ten minutes, we had a good chance of getting these guys.

We knew going in it was a dangerous part of town. Most of the enemy clan members, insurgents, gangsters, thieves, and thugs hung out down there. Black-market weapons and ammo were readily available and distributed throughout the Bokhara district of Mogadishu. Hence, well-armed bad guys would most certainly be waiting for us at the objective.

9

Side note on bad guys. They call them 'bad guys' for a reason. They tend to shoot at us. This is never preferred nor good.

The call to 'get it on' came at about 3:00 pm local. Tactically, this is 'no bueno' for one simple reason. The lights are on. They can see you. When the perps you are after have a history of shooting at you, it's also *preferred* they don't see you. This is why we would rather conduct a raid at night under the cover of darkness. We hold the advantage with high-tech night vision devices. But the enemy always gets a vote. We don't get to choose when and where they meet. This was a target of opportunity and time was of the essence.

Yes, we knew going in it would be tough. What we didn't know is by the time it was all done, nineteen of us would never make it back and another seventy-eight would be wounded. Even the fortunate minority who did not get shot, fragmented, or blown up would forever carry the emotional scars that are standard issue for the combat veteran. The body will heal itself in time. The heart and mind take a whole lot longer.

Some scars never go away. When you make it out of something where others did not, you will spend the rest of your life thanking those people who were on your left and on your right that day. I know the only reason I am still here today is by the grace of God and the efforts of those men. I will honor them both by proudly telling our story to all who will listen. As any survivor could attest, you will also find yourself forever struggling and haunted by an odd sense of guilt. Why me, God? Why did You let me live when others did not? Men who had families. Men who were three times the soldier I was. People who deserved to live. So why me?

You can let the guilt of 'why?' do one of two things. It can bury you in anger and pity. Or you can let it motivate you to live up to everything you're worth. Knowing your worth and realizing just how important you are to the big picture is a challenge, and something I struggle with even today. We are humans and we are magnificent at selling ourselves short.

Most of us want to make a difference in this world. We want to know at the end of the day we matter, that we counted for something. Those who wear the boots of the U.S. military need not worry about making a difference. It comes issued with the uniform. But for the rest of us out here in the real world we wonder, "How do *I* make a difference?" "What can *I* do that really matters?" "How will *I* be remembered?"

My friends, these are easy questions to answer if all you do is lead and lead by example. Because when you set an example for others to follow, those around you take notice. I promise you they do. Whether they tell you or not, they are watching. You lead, they will follow, and the team around you becomes stronger. Thus, you have made a difference and you have changed a life.

The Army manual on Military Leadership FM-22-100 has a simple definition for leadership: *Leadership is the process of influencing others to accomplish the mission by providing purpose, direction, and motivation.* It is a simple explanation, but exactly how you go about providing the purpose, direction, and motivation necessary to influence others is a topic that can fill thousands of books and millions of pages. I'm certainly not here to write another lesson on how to be a better leader. I just want you to be one.

The Ranger motto is 'Ranger's Lead the Way.' But they never told us leading others is dependent upon the position you hold. Notice at no point does the definition of leadership say anything about, rank, seniority, status, tenure, hierarchy, pay-grade, pecking order, totem poles, or ducks in a row. From the day you walked into the Ranger Regiment as a new ranger, you were told, "Leadership is the example you set for the people you serve."

We all serve somebody. There are always people to your left and to your right who are counting on you. It is your choice to deliver. I'm not telling you anything you don't already know. There is nothing new under the sun about leadership. You can go back to biblical times, and they were telling people the same things. For instance, when Paul the apostle sat alone for years in a Roman cell, he had some time on his hands. Instead of feeling sorry for himself, he used that time to do some good. He wrote a whole bunch of letters to folks who needed guidance on how to move forward leading this new thing called Christianity. In the most famous part of his letter to the Ephesians, he advises them to suit up for battle:

"Put on all of God's armor so that you will be able to stand firm against all strategies of the devil [or enemy]."
~ Eph. 6:11 (NLT).

To help illustrate the reality of spiritual warfare, Paul used stories from the modern-day battlefield of the Roman Empire to make his point. I will follow his lead. Because whether we are talking about the conquest of Germania, the Russian front, the beaches of Normandy, the mountains of Korea, the jungles of Vietnam, the streets of Mogadishu, Ramadi, or Kabul, the stories told by those who were there carry a common theme. Somebody, somewhere, at some terribly urgent moment and against all odds, did something extraordinary to lead the way. They set an example for others to follow. Be that person.

"The army taught me some great lessons—to be prepared for catastrophe—to endure being bored—and to know that however fine a fellow I thought myself in my usual routine, there were other situations...in which I was inferior to men that I might have looked down upon had not experience taught me to look up."~ Oliver Wendell Holmes Jr.

Whenever I get to walk on stage as a speaker for an event, I always make sure to tell the audience up front what I hope they get from the story. Tell people what you are 'gonna' tell them.

Then tell it to them. And then tell them what you just told them. This is how the Army taught us to give a block of instruction. Be crystal clear on what you want to communicate!

With that being said, here are four fundamental leadership truths I hope you remember from the stories I get to tell you in these next few pages:

Leadership is a choice
What you choose to do is always dictated by who you want to be.

Take care of your people
They are the most important asset you have available.

When we need you is when it's hard
When it's easy we can do it ourselves.

You have what it takes
We've all been told to 'surround ourselves with good people.' But we forget we are the 'good people' others have surrounded themselves with.

"Never shall I fail my comrades. I will always keep myself mentally alert, physically strong and morally straight. I will shoulder more than my fair share of the task, whatever it may be, 100% and then some."
~ 3rd Stanza of the Ranger Creed

It was supposed to have been a day off from training for the men of Task Force Ranger. We had been in Somalia for almost three months going nonstop day and night. If we weren't running a mission into the city, then we were busy training for one. Here it was October and finally we were catching a break. It was good to hear the boys laughing and enjoying the afternoon. Some of them were outside playing volleyball. Some were doing whatever it is they do on their downtime to kill time.

I was enjoying the personal time writing a letter home to my mom when the call rang out across the American compound. "Get it on!" A mission was coming down and it was time to gear up. Like firefighters running for their coats and helmets or fighter pilots scrambling to their jets, men dropped what they were doing and hustled toward their weapons to begin the transformation from soldier to superman.

"Dear Mom, You would love it here in sunny Mogadishu! It looks just like Ft. Lauderdale. I'll have to finish this letter a little later. We just got a call. Nothing to worry about. Probably a false alarm. Love, Keni."

I was wrong. Fifteen minutes later I was locked and loaded on board a special operations helicopter screaming along the Somali coastline at just five hundred feet off the deck. I sat in the open door, knees to the breeze, with the Indian Ocean gleaming beneath me in the late afternoon sun. As the shadow of the helicopter glided off the turquoise water, up over the dingy beach, and into the urban sprawl of the third-world slums below, the thoughts I enjoyed just moments before of home in Florida and Mom's pecan pie were a lifetime away.

The Blackhawk is a violent machine. It's loud. It shakes. It tests the pilot as the main rotors go one way and the tail rotor goes another. Whereas an airplane is designed to smoothly lift off the ground and wants to fly up and away, the MH-60 feels more like a maverick stallion beating the air into submission. With two electronically-fed gatling guns sticking out the windows, it's a mean looking machine.

Skimming across the surface of the Indian Ocean, the awesome sight of those big black helicopters reaching the shoreline must have looked like a small armada of impending doom to the Somali militia, who were scattering into their positions and hastily preparing for our arrival.

The Delta and Ranger assault force was formidable, consisting of seventy-five Rangers and forty Delta soldiers who would be inserted by four MH-6 Little Birds and six MH-60 Black Hawks. There were also four AH-6J Little Bird gunships providing close air support. The ground convoy or Reaction Force was made up of about fifty men on a dozen vehicles that would rendezvous with us at the target building and provide our extraction.

My squad was onboard Super 66. That was the mission call sign of our helicopter nicknamed 'The Gunslinger'. Our job was to fast-rope in at the southwest corner of the target building in order to cover that sector.

We were Chalk 3 of four other helicopters full of rangers. Each 'chalk' would simultaneously rope in at the four corners of the building putting a big perimeter around the target. That way the Delta teams were free to do their jobs on the inside knowing we had their backs on the outside.

"Thirty seconds!" yelled Staff Sergeant Hargis. He was the crew chief on my side.

I couldn't really hear him over the rotors, but I didn't need to. We all knew the time was at hand because the bird began to flare kicking up a dust storm of dirt and debris. That's when I finally saw the target building through the dust cloud. We were roof top high about sixty feet above the street. I could see the other Blackhawks come to a hover a block over. I could see Little Birds touching down as Delta operators stepped off and stormed the building. I could see them throwing people to the ground. And I could hear the gunfire begin. Here we go...

"Ropes!"

Fast-roping is an expeditious method of insertion to get fifteen men out of a helicopter and on to the ground fast. The Blackhawks were too big to land in the street so they would hover above the roof tops. Two big three inch thick ropes get kicked out both sides of the aircraft.

Like Batman disappearing out of frame down the bat pole, I watched as my squad members zipped away one after the other and vanished into the cloud of brown. Gravity will gladly assist you out of any aircraft especially when you are weighted down with sixty-plus pounds of gear. Since you aren't harnessed or safe-tied in, it's very important to have a positive grip on the nylon braided rope before you commit.

The thirty seconds it takes to get everyone out of the helicopter, down the ropes and onto the ground are intense because that big ole target in the sky is quite vulnerable. Remember people are already shooting. Like a horse in the rain, that aircraft has to hover there and take it. For the pilots and crew those thirty seconds probably felt more like thirty minutes.

I was the last man out. As soon as my feet hit the street, Super 66 cut ropes, powered up and forward towards the safety of altitude. Insertion complete.

"Somebody ought to do something about that."
~ attributed to every person ever.

At first, the gunfire out in the street wasn't that bad. This may seem an oddly understated comment to make to those of us going to work here in the real world. Imagine the shock and surprise if someone started taking shots at you on your way to work this morning? But for us that day, it came as no surprise. In fact, it really wasn't all that bad for one simple reason. They were missing! Which again, is the preferred outcome if the bad guys you are after have a history of shooting at you.

I had an instructor in Ranger School who once put it all into perspective for me. He said, "Ranger Thomas, if someone shoots at you and misses, it's just like they never shot at you at

SOMEBODY OUGHT TO DO SOMETHING

all. So there's no real reason to get all excited. Stay calm and do your job." Good advice.

The mission was going like clockwork and mostly according to plan. I say mostly because there was an issue on the insertion. One of the men in Chalk 4 behind us, Private Todd Blackburn, lost his grip on the rope and plummeted sixty something feet to the ground, landing with a sickening thud. He broke his back, was knocked unconscious and out of the fight before it got started. Fortunately for young Private Blackburn, the Ranger medic, Doc Marcus Good, was right there to provide immediate care as was Sergeant First Class Bart Bullock, the Delta medic. Since we had planned and trained for a casualty on infill, the process of safely evacuating Blackburn was well executed. He would live to talk about it.

It took three Humvees and more than a couple men to move Todd. Historic hindsight would prove this moment to be the beginning of the unraveling of this battle. Less than a minute into the mission and we were already fighting Murphy.

Delta cleared the building from the top down, bringing out about two dozen prisoners. The trucks drove up and the prisoners were loaded on board. The trucks drove off which left about eighty of us consolidating at the target building. The prisoners took up more room on the vehicles than we had anticipated. And because three of the HUMVEES had driven off ahead of the convoy to evacuate Private Blackburn, there weren't enough vehicles to get us all out. We were told to hold in place. Our ride home was supposed to be arriving in a few minutes. Turns out it was a few minutes too long.

Super 61 was piloted by Chief Warrant Officer Cliff Walcott and Chief Warrant Officer Donovan 'Bull' Briley. As pilots, both men were legends in the special operations community. On board were the two crew chiefs manning the mini-guns and two Delta Force snipers, Staff Sergeant Dan Bush, and Sergeant First Class Jim Smith.

Super 61 had been flying low and slow in an over-watch flight pattern when it was struck in the tail by a rocket propelled grenade. The aircraft turned a full 360 in what seemed to be a somewhat controlled maneuver, but not really. The MH-60 was starting its autorotation, the automatic procedure for crash landings. The smoking aircraft lost altitude and disappeared into the buildings about a half mile to our northeast.

For those of us at the target building watching it all go down, we knew what it meant, but none of us could believe it. That's not supposed to happen. That's the 160th Special Operations Air Regiment up there. No way did a third-world clan of poorly trained thugs wearing flip-flops and football helmets just bring down the best of the best with a hundred dollar rocket. But there it was, right before our eyes. I can describe for you what we were all feeling because you've felt the exact same thing. It's that knot you get in your stomach when life hits hard.

I know there are people reading this who lost loved ones during the pandemic and never saw it coming. "Hey Dad's in the hospital. You need to get here now." It's the same terrible feeling you might know if, God forbid, something happens to your children. And it's the same feeling everyone in this nation felt who watched the news on September 11, 2001.

When life hits unexpectedly, as it most certainly will, you would think and feel exactly what we were thinking as we watched Super 61 spinning hard into the buildings....

"I can't believe this is happening."

This momentary disbelief is a natural human reaction. The shock of the situation stops us in our tracks as our brain tries to make sense of what our eyes and ears are telling us.

We don't want to believe there's an officer and chaplain walking up to our front door, because it's not supposed to happen. We don't want to believe the hurricane we've been watching on the news for days is actually going to flood this city, because it's not supposed to happen. We don't want to believe the surgeon who just told us the tumors have spread far more aggressively than predicted and there's nothing more he can do. That's not supposed to happen.

But it is happening. The sooner we can come to grips with the fact that it's happening to us, the sooner we can realize it's also happening to those around us. Very rarely does anyone go through hardship alone. Others are always affected as well. Sometimes, that's our co-workers, our teammates and our neighbors. Most of the time it's our family and friends, people who care about us. Once you realize others are sharing in your hardship, you then have a choice to make. What are you going to do?

When talking to an audience, it's at this point in the story where I pause and explain how it would be very easy for me to strike a coaching stance with my hands on my hips, do the NCO chop and throw out a blanket statement about what a leader must do.

"Do the right thing!"

But I am very careful with my words. 'Do the right thing' is far too broad and too easy a solution to a very difficult moment. If I were to ask each of you to write down what you think 'the right thing' is, I would get many different answers dependent upon vast differences in personalities, culture, values, and beliefs. So instead of 'Do the right thing' I ask people in the audience,

"Who do you want to BE in that moment?"

Ultimately, what you do in any given situation is always an actionable choice influenced by who you want to be.

If you grew up in the culture of servant leadership like the Rangers, then you know exactly who you want to be and what you will do. Your mindset of putting the mission and others before yourself will dictate, giving you purpose. Your contingency planning, and training for such situations will provide direction. When the purpose and direction are clear, proper motivation always follows. No one needed to motivate us to move towards the crash and into the hornet's nest. We reacted and started moving in accordance with the contingency plan already in place.

Remember, leadership is the art of providing, purpose, direction, and motivation to accomplish the mission for the greater good of the organization. If the person you want to be is the transformational leader who serves others, then you too will move forward to help. We see it time and time and time again. People who believe they are part of something bigger than just themselves, will be the people that move towards the fray to help. When the cause is greater than oneself, people will step up for each other. They will be the leader we all want to follow.

So why is it when something tough is going down and life is hitting hard, we only hear of a few who stepped up and played the hero? Why is it most people do not? Think about it. In the past decade alone, we've read far too many terrible stories of active shooters firing rampantly into the innocent at school systems, concerts, movie theaters, churches, and grocery stores.

Every now and then you hear about the guy who, by himself, charged the shooter, bringing an end to the onslaught. Where were the others? What were they doing? I get running and taking cover when you hear shots fired. That's reactive. But where did everyone go when others were down? Wouldn't you expect everyone to help in whatever capacity they could? A handful of first responders, off-duty cops or military personnel are usually the ones getting mentioned in trying to organize the chaotic aftermath. Why is it ALWAYS, only the few who move immediately to help?

Now I do not believe for one second people are cowards. For the most part, we-the-people are raised to be a heroic lot. We want to try to 'do the right thing' if we can. But Americans, however special we may be, still fall under the category of human. And as humans we are magnificent at selling ourselves short.

The fundamental truth is that most people do not believe they have what it takes to actually make a difference, nor do they believe they have something to offer that really matters. So they default to doing nothing. And nothing accomplishes two things: Diddly and squat. The math is absolutely clear. Nothing begets nothing. $0 + 0 = 0$.

BEWARE! Before we begin pointing the finger of hypocrisy at others, we must appreciate that 'nothing' is a deceptive and insidious saboteur. This is because it usually starts with the best of intentions, but intentions are not the same as actions, are they?

Doing nothing starts like this…

"OMG! There's a helicopter going down!"

Then the back peddling begins. "Oh no! This is terrible. I hope they are 'gonna' be OK!"…more back peddling. And it always ends with –

"Somebody ought to do something about that!"

I can preach on this with authority because I catch myself saying the exact same thing at times in my life. "Man, somebody ought to do something about that." And then that higher voice in my head chimes in,

"Yeah Keni, SOMEBODY ought to do something. What can you do? Who are you 'gonna' be in this moment?"

U-U-G-G-H-H-H! I hate it when that voice is right!

21

Sometimes the person I want to be, doesn't always want to do what needs to be done. Because it means I'm going to have to do something difficult. I am going to have to put myself aside and put the needs of others before mine. I have to show up. I have to be present. Something is required of me which makes me responsible and accountable. Being responsible and accountable to others can get downright uncomfortable because I might just fail. Failure is fueled by fear. Fear is a powerful adversary. The hard right is called the hard right for a reason.

We have a saying in our family we use when we find ourselves complaining or whining about having to do things we don't want to do. In all honesty, the one doing the complaining is most often me. So Heidi gives me a little dose of perspective as a reminder...

"There's a Blackhawk going down, Keni...who do you want to be in this moment?"

That usually shuts me up.

I find it disappointing when I hear people deflect their responsibility to others by selfishly declaring "I'm not comfortable with this." Well of course you're not. But this is exactly when we need you; when it's hard. People don't need your help if it's comfortable and easy.

Most likely, no one is shooting at us today. Those kind of life and death situations, while very real, are still very rare in our day to day. But it is life. And it will go down. I can't tell you when or where, but I can tell you with absolute certainty life will hit hard one day. And when it does, remember to take a breath. Take a look to your left and right. Who else is struggling? Then ask yourself who do you want to be in that moment?

We don't have to be happy about the soup-sandwich we inherit. But we do have to own it. Because if we don't, who will? This is not a rhetorical question. The answer is...someone else.

When we don't step up in difficult situations, we leave it to someone else. That someone else is almost always the people to our left and our right. Our co-workers. Our family. Our friends. Our countrymen. As I explained to my kids when they were little, there are no magic elves waiting to clean up your mess. Likewise, there is no 'Someone else' reserve force coming to fight the fight for you.

"I didn't ask for this," you might say. I understand. No one asks for hard times. "It's not my responsibility." Maybe so. But it is now.

"It's not my fault," says every politician ever. It may not be your fault, but it is your problem. And since you don't seem to be doing anything about it Senator, it now means we have to.

In October of 2022, Hurricane Ian slammed into Southwest Florida as a Category 4 hurricane. It was the second most destructive hurricane to ever hit the state of Florida. Ever. Ian killed hundreds, destroyed billions, and instantly added thousands to the homeless population of the state.

The hurricane left one particular group of Floridians in a dire situation. Every person on Sanibel Island was cut off from the mainland and stranded when the three mile concrete causeway that was once a bridge was uprooted and destroyed by the storm.

Now think about the traffic construction in your hometown and how long it takes to complete a typical roadside project. Can you imagine the enormous undertaking required to replace a section of a highway bridge standing in the Gulf of Mexico? The planning and the financing alone would take at least a year. And that's just to get construction started.

But the citizens of Sanibel were in trouble. People were in need. Somebody needed to do something. So heroes rushed to help. An armada of boats and aircraft carrying supplies, generators and food came to the rescue. For weeks they kept up the brigade of help. Who piloted those planes? Who captained those boats? The citizens of Florida. That's who. The very same citizens who suffered through the very same storm put their own struggle aside and moved to help others. This is an example set by a servant leader mindset.

It's worth mentioning the leadership in place at the Florida governmental level. Their planning and forethought for disaster contingencies was impressive and set the example for others to follow. Because hurricanes are a fact of life in Florida, destruction is a very real possibility. There'd better be a contingency plan in place and rehearsed. Because if something goes down and you are not ready, you have already failed. In the arena of natural disasters, lack of planning and execution costs lives. People will suffer because of poor planning and poor decision making. Fortunately for those living on an island called Sanibel, the state was ready and came running.

Within days after the storm, construction crews already over-extended throughout the region, descended upon the project of rebuilding in order to rescue. Bridge building over water requires very specific equipment and highly capable engineering. It was there. By the end of October the bridge was repaired, and the stranded community was freed. It only took three weeks.

As I mentioned earlier, the servant leadership mindset of putting others before oneself will kick in and step up, providing purpose. Contingency planning and training for such situations will provide direction. When the purpose and direction are clear, proper motivation always follows.

Contrast the way Florida's leadership responded to Hurricane Ian with the way Louisiana's leadership responded after Hurricane Katrina sunk the city of New Orleans in 2005. As the flood waters stranded thousands, the fear-ridden leaders of The Big Easy got on camera immediately pointing a finger, blaming and whining about how "somebody else ought to do something about this."

This response is not an example set for others to follow. This is not a servant leadership mindset. It is a waste of time and a distraction from the matter at hand: people are in trouble. There will be a time for fault finding and holding people accountable. But that time will be later. Now is the time for a leader to step up and serve though active leadership, giving purpose and intent to those in despair. In their moment of need, the only thing you are accountable to should be the people you are supposed to be helping.

It was poor planning. Any direction the state should or could have given the people of New Orleans was ill-prepared and non-existent. Without purpose or direction, there was little motivation to help each other. Clean up and rebuilding drug on for years as the state of Louisiana looked for someone else to do something. We don't have to be happy about the soup sandwich we inherit. But by God we do have to own it. Because if we don't, who will?

As the transformational leader we are all striving to become, do we want to be the person who puts the struggle off on someone else? Would a team of servant leaders who put their people and their mission before themselves really want to pass the buck and choose to do nothing? Or would they rather be part of the solution by making a choice to take action? Should the conversation ever turn to blame or looking for someone else to do something about your problems, remember to ask yourself this.

"Who do I want to be in this moment?"

Because who you want to *be* will drive what you do.

And each man stands in the face of the light of his own drawn sword. Ready to do what a hero can.
~ Elizabeth Barrett Browning

First Lieutenant Tom Ditomasso was in a position to help. As God would have it, Lieutenant Ditomasso and his men were only four blocks away, on the very same street, where they saw the Blackhawk helicopter spiral into the ground. Tom immediately made a decision to move his team towards the crash in order to help the surviving crew who were already under attack from the mob. He called in his intentions to higher and was surprisingly told to stay where he was. Higher was evidently basing their decision on a more conservative plan of 'let's wait for back up.' But Lt. Ditomasso saw the urgency of the situation. He had a perspective the decision makers did not have. He knew the crew of Super 61 would not survive without help. His sense of duty to his comrades outweighed the order he had just been given to stay put. Lt. Ditomasso made a compromise. He left half his men where they were to fulfill the original obligation of keeping that area of the battlefield covered and secured. He took the other half of his men and ran towards the crash.

Outnumbered ten to one, Tom and his men moved under fire to the wreckage arriving just in time to save one of the crew members from certain death. Lt. Tom Ditomasso would later be awarded the Silver Star for his valor that day. He was also fired by his commander for disobeying an order.

Doing the right thing doesn't always work out in our favor does it? Sometimes they will alienate and ridicule you. Sometimes they will reprimand or defile you. Sometimes they will nail you to a cross. But duty and service to others requires the personal courage to willingly accept full responsibility for your actions and performance. If you ask Tom today what would he have done differently back then in retrospect, he will tell you...

"I would do nothing differently. When I looked at the crowd of Somalis who were sprinting towards the crash, I knew we had no choice. If any of our guys were still alive, they were going to need our help. I looked at the men I trusted looking back at me, and they all agreed, we had to move and move fast."

Tom Ditomasso is a hero in my book. I wish more of our elected officials had half the personal courage of that man.

Courage is not necessarily the absence of fear; it is the ability to put fear aside and do what is necessary or right in that moment both physically and morally.
~ Army Field Manual FM22-100

There's a scene in the Disney/Pixar movie *Planes 2* where the hero Dusty Crophopper is struggling to find his personal courage. Like all good stories, the hero must face and overcome his fears if he is to become a hero at all. Dusty wants to get certified as a firefighter for all the right reasons. But in order to do so, he has to push himself outside of his self-perceived limitations. To do what must be done in the heat of battle, Dusty Crophopper has to redline his engine and thus run the risk of blowing it up never to fly again. Dusty's mentor is a battle hardened veteran of firefighting appropriately named Blade Ranger!

During the midst of a crisis situation, Dusty begins to fall victim to the fear of self-doubt. *"You can do this. You have to do this!"* Blade implores. But Dusty uses his fragile gear box injury as an excuse to do nothing. Fortunately for Crophopper, he has a leader who has built a culture of servant leadership. Blade Ranger knows what it takes to bear the burden of living up to values like honor, integrity, and duty.

As the flames close in, Dusty Crophopper is ready to quit and let someone else handle the situation, Blade Ranger hits him with these words of motivation.

"Life doesn't always work out the way you want it to. But if

you quit today, think of all the lives you won't save tomorrow...
What are you gonna do?"

There's a Blackhawk going down. Who do you want to be?
When Super 61 crashed into the ground somebody had to come
into the pattern to replace the loss of our overhead close air
support. The pilots of Super 64 Chief Warrant Officer Mike
Durant, Chief Warrant Officer Ray Frank, and their two crew
chiefs were in a hold north of the city when they got the call.
Mike came into the pattern and began orbiting the battle
space around the target building. He barely had time to get his
bearings when he too was hit by an RPG. The rocket clipped
the tail rotor.

At first, it seemed structurally, the aircraft was holding together
and Super 64 would be able to make it back to the airfield.
But the blast did more damage than first thought. It didn't take
long for the tail rotor, churning away at 1,200 revolutions per
minute, to come apart. With nothing left to counter the main
rotors and keep the aircraft straight, the once gravity-defying
machine was forced into an irreversible spin. Impact with the
ground was eminent. Chief Durant had just enough time to
radio their status in typical Night Stalker fashion—matter of
fact, cool, calm, and collected.

"Six-four is going in. Six-four is going in."

Super 64 crashed a mile away from the main force falling into a
shanty town full of shacks, slums, and Somalis hell-bent to kill
whatever Americans might still be alive. What moments before
was an invincible special operations MH-60, was now reduced
to a collapsed and smoking heap of fuselage only vaguely
resembling a helicopter.

Miraculously all four crew members survived the crash. The
two pilots were badly injured and still strapped into their
collapsed seats. Mike's back was broken, and Ray Frank
was unconscious. The two crew chiefs Tommy Field and Bill

Cleveland were no better. Someone up in the reconnaissance aircraft had reported seeing Tommy briefly sit up then fall back into the bay. According to Mike Durante's recollection, Bill Cleveland was 'tore up pretty bad' from the wreckage. None of these aviators were in any condition to defend their ground. Bad guys were moving in quickly with a deadly head start on any kind of rescue force that could be sent. The situation was as urgent as it gets.

The only people left in a position to provide any sort of immediate help were the seven men aboard Super 62, one of the last Blackhawks left in the sky. On board were three Delta Force snipers. Master Sergeant Gary Gordon and Sergeants First Class Randy Shughart and Brad Halling. Their job had been to provide covering fires during the initial raid for the guys on the ground. That job description was about to change.

From their vantage point hovering above the wreckage, the men could clearly see the scene below going from bad to worse. With the inevitability of an oncoming stampede, hundreds of armed militia and an angry mob of Somalis were racing toward the incapacitated crew. If anyone was going to make it in time to rescue the downed airmen, Gordon, Shughart and Halling were the only ones in a position to do so. They coordinated a hasty plan.

Chief Warrant Officer Mike Goffena, the pilot, called in the situation report requesting to insert the Delta team and stressing the urgency of the situation. They were denied.

Goffena repeated the request this time emphasizing the fact he could see movement inside the wreckage meaning someone was still alive. Somalis were starting to move in. Denied.

Apparently, saving the lives of the survivors was not worth the risk of losing another fourteen million dollar aircraft and its crew. When you are the guy making those kinds of decisions from the relative safety of a high orbiting command aircraft, I suppose your risk assessment seems logical and justified. But when you are a Delta sniper sitting on the floor of a screaming helicopter just a few hundred feet above the gunfight where your comrades wait in dire need of help, risk assessment is not something you think about with detached logic.

You do what needs to be done right then and there, because someone is counting on you.

At this point, MSG Gary Gordon got on the radio to repeat the insertion request.

"Lemme speak to the Actual." Gordon called, meaning he wanted to speak directly to the actual person making the decision.

Gary Gordon made his intent clear...

"Gary, do you know what you're asking us?" came the reply.

The last words anyone would ever hear Gary Gordon say were,

"Sir, we're their only hope."

This time, Super 62 was finally given the go to insert. Chief Goffena picked an open spot about a hundred meters from the crash. As he flared to touch down, the repercussions were immediate. The bird came under heavy small-arms fire. Somalis were now firing from every roof top with everything they had. Each tink-tink-tink on the side of his aircraft meant a few more rounds punctured the thin skin and was wreaking havoc with its mechanical innards. To a helicopter pilot forced to sit tight on the ground while people are shooting, time moves backward. He's thinking, "We 'gotta' go, and we 'gotta' go like yesterday!"

The starboard side crew chief was fully engaged on the mini gun covering the insertion when he got hit. SFC Brad Halling, one of the Delta operators, leaped behind the gun as it was their heaviest casualty producing asset available. One machine gun and two sniper rifles. It wasn't much of a rescue team and certainly not the preferred show of force against an enemy contingency of two hundred moving in. The guardians from above descended out of the heavens and into a living hell.

Once Shughart and Gordon were on the deck, Goffena immediately lifted off to escape the increasing barrage of bullets. But just like during the initial insertion, the brownout and rotor wash was choking and disorienting. As the big helicopter pulled away, the dirt kicked up like a giant dust devil and neither of the Delta operators was sure which way to move. Shughart signaled up to the pilots asking for the direction of the crash.

Ignoring the tink-tink-tink once again, Chief Goffena willingly took his bird back down to the ground to help show the way for the disoriented snipers. He actually pointed out the window to guide the two men. The crew chief threw out a smoke grenade in the direction of the downed aircraft. The operators gave a thumbs-up as Super 62 once more, pulled away to provide covering fire.

Taking full responsibility for their own actions, knowing they were astronomically outnumbered, and that backup would not be coming any time soon, Gary Gordon and Randy Shughart sprinted towards the wreckage and into a hail of gunfire.

Under intense small arms fire and with complete disregard for their own safety, Gordon and Shughart fought their way to crash site two. Brad Halling and the crew of Super 62 circling above were doing all they could to provide support when an RPG ripped a hole in the left side of the aircraft, forcing Goffena to head back to the airfield. Task Force Ranger lost another Blackhawk. Brad Halling would lose his leg in the explosion. Shughart and Gordon would lose what little help they had. The two men were on their own.

One by one, the snipers methodically held off the advancing militia. With steady rhythm and lethal accuracy, they fired round after round after round. Remember, they were Delta operators. They did not miss. This should give you some idea of the numbers they were up against. They fired and fired until there were no more rounds to be fired. With nothing left to protect them, they were overrun and killed. The modern battlefield is not a video game. Weapons run out of ammunition. Men die and do not come back to life.

When it was all over, Mike Durant the pilot would be the only survivor. Mike was taken captive that day. We got him back eleven days later. His is a story of faith, brotherhood, and perseverance. He will tell you; he owes his life to those two men. Read his book, *In the Company of Heroes*. It will inspire you.

Master Sergeant Gary Gordon and Sergeant First Class Randy Shughart would later be honored posthumously with the Congressional Medal of Honor. It's the only time in the history of that award where the two citations for both men read exactly alike. When I tell you it is an honor and a privilege to tell the story of Task Force Ranger, I mean it from the bottom of my heart.

Gary Gordon had a choice to make. Randy Shughart had a choice to make. Even Brad Halling the third Delta sniper onboard Super 62 had a hard choice to make. There is no doubt everything in Brad was screaming to move into the fray alongside his buddies. But at 4000 rounds per minute, the rotating barrels of the mini gun were the best option to support his team.

It would have been an understandable out to simply follow orders and abort any sort of rescue attempt. Why would men, without hesitation, put their life on the line for someone they barely knew? I can promise you they didn't even know the names of the crew members they were trying to save. So it wasn't due to a friendship connection. They could have waited for backup. They could have just followed instructions to stay out of harm's way. So it wasn't because they were simply 'following orders' as many may assume is how the military works. What was the motivating factor then? What cause could be so great?

If Gary or Randy were alive I know exactly what they would say: "Because they would have done it for me."

It really is that simple.

"I will never leave a fallen comrade to fall into the hands of the enemy."
~ the fifth stanza of the Ranger Creed

When your entire culture is all about service to one another, the responsibility to help your mates becomes an absolute commitment and an unbreakable promise. No one takes the hill alone. Rangers, Delta, Special Forces, SEALS, we all know this. So team inter-dependence rather than individualism becomes the norm. When men and women are accountable to one another, they will do what must be done regardless of the circumstance. In other words, those who believe they are part of something bigger than themselves will be the ones to step up when it's hard. And when it's hard, is exactly when we need you.

Becoming a transformational leader requires more than a desire to better serve others. It requires intentional action like showing up time and time again. It asks the best of you in the worst of times. You can't get it on an app. You can't order it from Amazon for same day delivery. It's neither convenient nor easy. And that's exactly why it will mean something to you! Think about it. The accomplishments we value the most are the ones we worked hardest to achieve.

If Ranger school were a fun, feel-good summer camp experience, the ranger tab I get to wear on my shoulder would mean very little. For instance, when you sign up to bring your team through the Downrange Leadership Development Course it will not be easy. But you will come out on the other end of those three days with your head held high, confident in your ability to lead through adversity. And long after the blisters heal and your muscles stop aching, your heart will remember with pride the depth of your accomplishment.

It bears repeating. This leadership path you are on will get difficult at times. The responsibility of leading others requires intestinal fortitude because, why? Because when we need you is when it's hard. That's why. The good news is, the yellow brick road wasn't all lions and tigers and bears, oh my. You will meet like-minded souls and build a team of unique capabilities and talented individuals. You will learn to lead them to your objective and together you will overcome any enemy, adversity, hardship, or evil flying monkeys.

Why will you choose to persevere and endure the burden of leadership when others are falling by the wayside? Because your motivating factor is a powerful one of servitude. When you understand you are part of something bigger than yourself, your first responsibility is to those on your left and right in order to complete the mission. 'For each other' will become your purpose. You will find the personal courage in difficult times to set the example for others to follow.

"Recognizing I volunteered as a Ranger, fully knowing the hazards of my chosen profession…"
~ the first stanza of the Ranger Creed

Every morning at zero dark thirty, somewhere in the world, a group of Rangers are standing in formation. They are called to attention. The First Sergeant asks for 'six motivated individuals" to recite the Ranger Creed. There is a mad scramble out of the ranks as volunteer's race to the front. The first six to get there line up at the position of attention. Each man then recites one stanza out of six that make up the Ranger Creed and the entire company repeats it back.

It begins like this: "Recognizing I volunteered as a Ranger..."
...and the Rangers repeat, "Recognizing I volunteered as a Ranger..."

Gary Gordon and Randy Shughart knew exactly what they volunteered for when they made their request to be inserted. There was an overwhelming force of armed enemy clearly en route. But that came with the territory. That is what they signed up to do. Gary's wife Carmen knew without a doubt why her husband volunteered to do what no one in their right mind would have done.

"Gary was 100 percent Ranger. He lived the Ranger Creed. He went in there to help his fellow soldiers. Not to die."

"...Fully knowing the hazards of my chosen profession."
...and the Rangers repeat, "Fully knowing the hazards of my chosen profession."

Can you imagine if at home, or at your job, or in your school, you had a creed that you and your family or colleagues recite before the day begins? Something motivating that will inspire in you the will to fight for a cause that is bigger than yourself. A mission statement with a purpose to remind you why you are there and just how important you are. A testament that provides direction and screams to the world, "This is who I am, and this is where I am going. We're their only hope. Follow me!"

The point of saying a creed every day is to make it more than a bunch of words. You say it enough, you begin to believe it. You begin to believe it and you will start living it. I don't know if you have a creed to live by. A prayer, an oath, a pledge, or a solemn promise you repeat on a daily basis. Something that reminds you to be there for those you lead one hundred percent and then some. But if you need a good one, I've got one for you.

It's on the walls of the 75th Ranger Regiment. It's on the walls of the Delta Force compound in Fort Bragg, North Carolina. It's on the walls of the 160th Special Operations Air Regiment, the SEAL Team locker rooms, and the Air Force special operations command in Tampa, Florida. In fact, it's on the walls of every single one of our special operations units out there. It's from the Old Testament of the Bible:

Then I heard the voice of the Lord saying, "Whom shall I send? And who will go for us?" And I said, "Here am I. Send me!"
~ Isaiah 6:8 (NIV)

I don't get to wear the uniform of the 75th Ranger Regiment anymore. I don't get to stand shoulder to shoulder and hold the line with the greatest men this country has ever known. I no longer carry a rifle. I do get to stand on a stage with a microphone in hand. Both have a working end. Both can make an impact. My mission is no longer raids and reconnaissance. But you can still send me. I can tell a story. I can sing a song. These are the gifts I have been given. And you can count on me to use them to the absolute best of my ability.

I could never know all that is required of you in your chosen calling or profession. But I do know whatever it is you do; you are better equipped for it than I am. This is why to every audience I get a chance to speak for, I thank them. "Thank you for what you do, for raising your hand. Thank you for doing something I cannot, and what most others aren't willing to try. You have been sent."

But remember this. Once you step forward and say "Send me. Put me in coach. Give me the job. You can count on me," you have now become part of something much larger than yourself.

You have now become part of a thing called a team, where someone to your left and to your right are always counting on you. You are the 'good people' others have surrounded themselves with.

Like a superhero ready to do what is right, you have accepted what a leader must be, know and do. You have everything you need to attack the challenges others shy away from. Your character is rock solid, and God is on your side. So drive on to the Ranger objective and complete the mission though you be the lone survivor. Push forward in the face of adversity while shouting out to those around you, "Follow Me!" Lead the way with purpose, direction, and motivation even if the only person you are leading is yourself!

One last thing. Leadership is a choice. Take care of your people. When we need you is when it's hard. You have what it takes. You see what I did there?

"To every man there comes in his lifetime that special moment when he is tapped on the shoulder and offered the chance to do a very special thing, unique to him and fitted to his talents. What a tragedy if that moment finds him unprepared and unqualified for the work which would be his finest hour." ~ Winston Churchill

---

Endnotes

The Downrange Advanced Leadership school is an outdoor three-day, intensive leadership and team building experience. Our servant-leadership model of 'My People and My Mission, before Myself' is a mindset that is taught and lived by our decorated combat operators from the Special Operations community, Army Rangers and Special Forces commandos. We employ the ranger-school doctrine of teaching small unit troop-leading procedures in a highly-challenging, outdoor tactical environment.

Downrange is a transformational opportunity for your team to train side by side with special operators and become the type of leaders men and women will want to follow! If you think you are ready to take on that challenge then come train with us.

Watch the Emmy award winning video: http://downrangers.com

About Keni

As a member the 3rd Ranger Battalion, Sergeant Keni Thomas was deployed to Mogadishu, Somalia as part of a special operations group called Task Force Ranger. Their mission was to find and capture a criminal warlord named Mohammed Farrah Aideed. Outnumbered 10 to 1, the men of TFR distinguished themselves in an 18-hour fire fight that would later be recounted in the highly successful book and movie *Blackhawk Down*. In this TFR strike, 19 Americans died and 78 were wounded.

Keni got out of the Army to pursue a successful country music career. He is an Emmy-winning producer, a best-selling author and still regularly tours with the USO to perform for our military personnel serving overseas. As an entertainer, Keni has been recognized by Congress and the White House for his dedicated work on behalf of our veterans and military families. Keni now travels globally as a motivational speaker. His message of servant leadership and teamwork inspires and challenges us to become the kind of leader others want to follow.

Keni is very proud to be a national spokesperson for the Special Operations Warrior Foundation which provides college educations to the children of our special operations personnel killed in combat or training. Keni Thomas is a graduate of the University of Florida, a recipient of the American Patriot Award and the Bronze Star for Valor.

CHAPTER 2

NAVIGATING THE LEADERSHIP BATTLEFIELD

BY MAJOR (Retired) ANDREW E. WHITE

According to some experts, the qualities of leadership are mostly learned. I've read that roughly 25% of leadership skills are innate while 75% are learned. That's good news because even those who do not aspire to lead are capable of learning leadership skills that will benefit themselves as well as influence others in positive ways throughout their lives. That's a win-win. Leadership, whether on an actual battlefield or in the business world begins on the inside.

Leadership has everything to do with morality. Motivation dictates morality. If you're going to be a leader, if that is your desire or calling in life, you must know what it is that you want to accomplish as a leader and why. You must develop a plan and consciously and deliberately direct your course. It is my desire to provide some help and guidance here as you begin or continue your journey.

RESPECT, EMPATHY AND CARE ARE INTEGRAL LEADERSHIP QUALITIES

To successfully be the leader of a troop of military men and women, a team – be it a sports team, political or corporate team – a family, or a congregation, you need to inspire the people looking to you to show the way. If you expect any individual or group of people to help you achieve your goals, you must be capable of, and devoted to, helping them reach their highest aspirations. A leader only leads by setting an example. So, you must understand going in that you can set a good example or a bad example. It's your choice.

How will you, as a leader, inspire others? While the place of business, boardroom or conference room may not look like a battlefield, the lives and wellbeing of many are at stake in how any business is conducted. Earning respect is crucial, as is showing that you care about the work of those in your business or on your team. You earn respect by showing respect. You get those under your leadership to care about you by showing that you care about them. Good and great leaders are empathetic. True leaders never put people down. Instead, they build everyone up around them and make people understand and feel their value and worth.

I had to earn the respect of an entire troop on a second tour of duty in the Sinai Peninsula. I arrived to what can only be called a complete breakdown in leadership. The members of the troop were behaving irresponsibly. Without getting into the details, suffice it to say they were acting like they were on holiday instead of being a protective presence in a hostile environment. I had to find a powerful way to teach each member of the troop that they are always accountable for their actions. I had to earn their respect while also getting them to understand that their behavior was putting lives in danger, civilian lives as well as the lives of their fellow troop members and battle buddies.

One night while touring the base shortly after my arrival, I found several of the unit members sleeping in the tower while on night patrol. This is totally unacceptable behavior and a clear representation of a breakdown in leadership. I had to get to know what made each member of the team tick. I didn't have much time to get everyone on the same page. I spent each night in the tower with the night patrol. I took meals with the troops. I learned what each person was really interested in. I found out if they were married and had children back home, their birthdates, what they aspired to in life. After a week, I had the entire troop do an exercise that woke them up and made them understand how critical it was for them to be fully responsible for their actions. They had to maintain a battle-ready stance, which meant being alert, and conscientious of their actions and responsibilities at all times. This troop ultimately turned out to be a stellar example of how people, when given the right example, when they know their leader has their back and genuinely cares about their well-being and that they have value, how it brings out the very best character traits.

WHAT MAKES PEOPLE TICK

The secret weapon of great leaders is getting to know the people under their command. There are good leaders who are successful, but genuinely caring about people takes you to the level of greatness. During one of my tours of duty, I had a soldier who was very interested in mechanics. He was a car-nut kind of guy. He just loved working on any kind of vehicle, pretty much anything with a motor. I took every opportunity I had to send him to help on that kind of job. Other members of the troop asked me why that soldier *had* to do that job. They knew it wasn't his 'job.' My answer was always the same. "He doesn't *have* to do it. He loves to do it. He's in his element."

My goal as a leader has always been to find out what the people around me like the most and will get their mind off whatever negative situation might arise and keep them focused on accomplishing the mission at hand. Of course, there are going to be introverts in any group, but it's the job of the leader to find out what gets them to tick too. Ask basic questions. Even the most closed off person will give you clues. Find out what they do on their off time. Find out how they dress when they are on their own time.

Getting to know what makes your people tick will show them that you care. Notice how they behave. Do they go to the barracks and read a book instead of hanging out with others? What kind of books do they read? What kind of music do they like and listen to? What kind of sports teams do they follow? What kind of pictures do they have on their desk? Great leaders are like good detectives. They keep digging to find out the smallest things about their people to spark a conversation.

Ask questions, lots of questions about the people around you. Not deep personal questions, but questions that find a positive trigger. You must find out how to get that kind of information out of them, so they know you believe in them. That's when they will believe in you and support you wholeheartedly.

See, that's the crucial part. The people under your leadership in any group or organization must know that you believe in them and will stand by them. I do the same thing in business that I did in the military. I get to know my people, who they are, what they like, what they dislike. You cannot be a great leader if you know nothing about the people you are meant to be inspiring to great acts of creativity, boldness, or courage, while in some cases risking their lives for a greater good.

NOBODY WORKS FOR ME – EVERYBODY WORKS WITH ME

Whenever your behavior directly affects the lives of others you cannot have questionable morals. Not long after I arrived on that second tour of duty in the Sinai Peninsula, when morale was the lowest of all 4 troops when I took over and, after I had taught my troop responsibility for their every action, I was called to a meeting. I was asked by my commanding officer, "Captain White, why have I not heard of one issue with your men?" My response was based on my leadership promise. I told my commanding officer. "Minus criminal, or illegal activities, Sir, we take care of issues internally. We control what happens inside our unit."

Our troops on duty in the Sinai Peninsula were dealing with life and death situations. Just down the road from our base, nine people were killed in a car bombing. This is real life in many places in the world. Life is not a joke. This kind of extreme activity puts things in perspective. When your troop, your team, your family, your political party, your congregation knows you have their backs and when they know they are going to be held accountable and responsible for their actions, you've got a great team.

Napoleon had a corporal diplomacy policy. Before he would ever brief his generals regarding a battle plan, he first brought in a young corporal and explained it to him. If the young corporal understood his plan, he would brief his generals. Napoleon got to know the men under his command this way. Corporate leaders must do the same.

Far more often than anyone would like to admit, many leaders are too quick to start pointing fingers at others when something goes wrong. The way I see things, a leader facing any issue must be the first one to take responsibility. I recommend asking yourself, where were you as the leader who failed to make sure whoever you're pointing the finger at had the tools and motivation to get things done? The finger can only point to me if there is a breakdown or perceived failure that happens below me.

Each member of a troop or a team has a specific job to do. And every job is relevant from the bottom all the way up to the top. Yet, everyone sees the same situation differently based on their personal experience. I always met my young privates. I would have meals with them. I asked them where they were looking to go. I would spend hours with them in the towers…they got to know me, and I got to know them. If I know my people I can usually pinpoint where I missed an opportunity to avert an issue.

As I mentioned earlier, if the people you are meant to be leading don't have the right motivation and desire to get things done, then, the question is, exactly what are they doing and what the heck are you doing? Motivation dictates morals. Whether in the military or the civilian world, bad or questionable morals equate to bad or questionable motivation. In my opinion, the movie, *The Wolf of Wall Street* clearly depicts this. The lead character was a great motivator with very questionable morals.

I'm not suggesting that the CEO of a huge international corporation needs to know everyone in the company. If something goes wrong in a corporation, the CEO doesn't need to be bothered. Team leaders and managers take care of the little stuff. The CEO knows those in leadership positions who report up. The directors and managers and team leaders know those in supporting roles under their management. Whatever level of leadership you are in, you must earn the respect of those you lead. You simply cannot expect everyone to see things the way you do. A great example of this is Brad Paisley's song, *I'm Still A Guy*. One of his lyrics says, "When you see a priceless French painting, I see a drunk, naked girl." None of us can ever really walk a mile in anyone else's shoes. It's impossible. No one perceives any one situation the exact same way. The late Steven Covey, author of *The 7 Habits of Highly Effective People*, is noted as saying that "Strength lies in differences, not in similarities." I agree with Mr. Covey. As leaders, we must know how to inspire, draw out, and make use of the different talents, skills, and abilities of those around us to create the strongest, most effective teams.

LEADERS VS. BOSSES

Early in my military career, a colleague and I had a leader that was more of a boss than a leader. I thought he would greet the team members. I was wrong, Not only did this 'leader' not give guidance to his team, but he also gave nothing of himself. This unit leader was marked by his superiors as 'need's leadership guidance.' He did not take that information to heart and consequently did not make it very far in the military. I've been able to develop three exceptional leaders from the same team that this leader nearly destroyed.

One was a good friend and colleague of mine who was close to getting kicked out of the military because of the lack of attention and leadership. This fellow was in a second leadership position but was under the command of the person who considered himself a 'boss.' I made it my business to find a way to get this guy into the proper school to get the right kind of education for his military career. I taught him, encouraged, and motivated him. Today he is head of intelligence.

It's not about your success as a leader. It's about the success of the people around you. Leaders build legacies which go well beyond any awards and accolades, it's about the leaders you develop and grow up around you. Look at coach trees of football teams for examples. And remember, toxic leaders can destroy not only morale but also a person's life and career.

Another good buddy of mine and I, during our first overseas tour, had two of the worst leaders possible. They were the kind of leaders who wanted lots of attention. Their attitude was that of "Look at me. See what's on *my* chest. See what's on *my* sleeve." They did not care about the men around them. When we were getting unit shirts out of the 4 officers in the unit, only myself and my buddy were given shirts. These were team morale shirts to designate our unit. But the unit did not give those 2 leaders shirts.

When it came to housing one of these unit leaders, the team members made it clear to me they did not want him under the same roof. I oversaw securing housing and room assignments. I told him we didn't have any more room in the house. I put him in a barracks by himself making him think he was king. It took him a full 3 months to realize the men didn't want him anywhere around.

LEADERSHIP OPPORTUNITIES PRESENT THEMSELVES IN EVERYDAY LIFE

It is not just those with whom we work closely that we inspire. We inspire everyone in our environment whether they are under our command or not. Every receptionist and administrative assistant could be an extraordinary leader hiding in plain sight. If you have any interaction with someone, that someone is worth knowing. Case in point, we have an administrative assistant who has been with us for 41 years. She is the gatekeeper to a top executive. She is not my assistant, yet I know her favorite color, what kind of plants she adores, when her birthday is and more. You must know what makes your gatekeeping tick. After all they are the ones who dictate where you need to be and when you need to be there.

Family members are always providing opportunities to become better leaders. Recently my son gave me an opportunity to help him shift his thinking and learn a valuable lesson. We love playing golf together and he is on his high school golf team. He just got his first car and his first job. He told me he wanted to buy a rangefinder during Amazon days. He wanted me to go 50/50 with him on it. Instead of just saying no to him, I asked him "When you go play team golf are you allowed to use a range finder?" His answer, "No." I continued with more questions. First, I told him, you have money now, but if you spend money on that, how will you get gas money? He pushed back and said, "But you buy expensive things and still buy gas." I explained that I've been earning money since I was 12 years old. I've been earning for over 30 years in my career. I told him, "You have bills to pay. You'll appreciate it more when you spend the rest of the summer getting sustainable income." My point to my son is that challenge is what makes you and motivates you. If something is simply given to you, it has no value. My son understood that in life it's important to prioritize.

YOUR GREATEST TOOL FOR NAVIGATING THE LEADERSHIP BATTLEFIELD

As I hope you understand now, the first and most important tool you'll need as a leader is a mindset shift. Conquer your inner landscape, know why you want to lead and what motivates you. The world needs more great leaders. Imagine the good you can do when you provide the leadership others need to achieve greatness. A recent article spells it out. "Organizations with great bosses, on average, produce 147% higher earnings per share than their competitors. This boost comes from higher quality work, discretionary effort, and productivity. Great leaders leverage team diversity by creating safe environments where everyone feels comfortable. Managers must foster judgment-free environments and provide air cover, so employees feel comfortable letting down their guard. At that point, employees will offer up suggestions, and the team will benefit."

Expect the best from yourself. Show your team you believe in them. Get to know them and let them know you genuinely care about them. Under these circumstances, they will give you their best. And remember what I said at the beginning: Motivation is everything, even false motivation. By that I mean make someone believe they are the best at something even if they aren't. Make your people believe that you believe in them more than they do. Eventually they will believe in themselves as much as you do, and that can only lead to great things.

Resources:
  • https://www.inc.com/michael-schneider/only-10-percent-of-people-are-natural -leaders-rest-of-us-have-to-work-on-developing-these-3-qualities.html
  • https://www.gallup.com/workplace/231593/why-great-managers-rare.aspx

About Andrew

Major (Retired) Andrew E. White is from Fairfield, CT. At the age of five, he dressed up as a soldier for Halloween and started letting everyone know that was what he was going to be when he grew up. In 1994, Andrew enlisted in the U.S. Army. In 1996, he graduated from Roger Williams University with a BA in History and Political Science with a minor in Marketing. In 1998, Andrew was given the opportunity to become an officer in the US Army as a 2LT. In 2000, Andrew moved to Dallas, TX and became a member of the Texas Army National Guard 1/112 AR. Following the attacks on September 11, 2001, Andrew was quickly recalled to duty in support of Operation Noble Eagle where he was the XO for DFW airport. In 2004, 1LT/CPT White first deployed to Iraq where he served as the XO for H TRP 1/124 CAV.

Andrew White proudly calls Texas his home with his wife Katie and three children for over 20 years. Andrew White has served overseas in support of Operation Iraqi Freedom and Operation Enduring Freedom. He is an active member of multiple veteran organizations in the Dallas/ Fort Worth community, including the VFW, American Legion, Military order of World Wars, Navy League, and Dallas Veterans Day Parade. In 2011, Governor Rick Perry made Andrew an Honoree Admiral in the Texas Navy. In December of 2016, he was recognized as a U.S. Congressional Veteran Commendation recipient by then US Congressman Sam Johnson (R, 3rd District of TX)

Andrew has made a lifetime commitment of selfless service to his country and community as a tireless community leader, whether it is with the Military or his involvement with community events, such as the Dallas Veterans Day parade where he serves as the Military Liaison. He re-established the Oath of Enlistment ceremonies prior to the start of the parade. In 2012, Andrew White led the charge in organizing the "Freedom Road Project" where veterans laid down a Red, White, and Blue stripe on the parade route for the Veterans Day parade.

Andrew White serves his community development growth to promote Veteran-friendly organizations, companies, and Veteran topics through his radio show "Kilroy's Conversation" (heard only on KVGIradio.com).

In 2014, Andrew started and founded Kilroy's GI Contractors, a veterans

General Contracting company. Kilroy's GI hires veterans and families of veterans in order to fill skilled and unskilled residential home repair and remodeling positions. He provides high-level customer service and a veteran's attention to detail in every project they take on.

On January 2nd 2019, after 20 plus years of service, Andrew White retired from the United States Army.

CHAPTER 3

MISSION DRIVEN TO HELP OTHERS LIVE FEARLESSLY AND PROSPEROUSLY

BY CORY NEUMILLER

Prosperity means something different to everyone. Many people relate prosperity to having great wealth in the form of money and assets. That way of thinking typically leads people to believe that there is a quantifiable amount of money/wealth that will result in prosperity. They think there's a magic number for each person that would provide never-ending happiness, security, and immunity from ever having a bad day or having their feelings hurt.

We all know of or have heard about people who have a lot of money and are miserable. And, we also know or have heard of others who are not what society would consider wealthy by any stretch of the imagination, but who are happy and live fulfilling lives. Their wealth is measured by the fulfillment of their values, not by the value of their bank accounts.

The truth is that prosperity is much more than the acquisition of money or wealth. True prosperity includes joy, happiness, good health, inner peace, a sense of belonging and contributing.

It also includes the richness of experiences such as making of memories with family, friends and loved ones, time spent pursuing passions and hobbies. These are the building blocks of true and fulfilling prosperity.

People who achieve true prosperity reach a level of fulfillment in which they feel they have made significant contributions to the lives of others. These contributions certainly include, but are not exclusively, financial contributions.

THE GREATEST OBSTACLE THAT PREVENTS MOST PEOPLE FROM ACHIEVING PROSPERITY

In my experience, the biggest obstacle to prosperity is fear. Many people have been conditioned to be fearful about money and subsequently are unaware of how they prevent themselves from achieving financial prosperity. A friend and colleague shared with me the acronym she thinks of when fears rise in her mind: (F.E.A.R.) <u>False Evidence Appearing Real</u>.

I have been fortunate to have witnessed and experienced both prosperity and fear, along with their impact professionally as well as personally. As the owner and operator of a wealth management firm, my mission is to help my clients define and achieve their ideas of prosperity. Inevitably fear comes up in our early discussions.

Below is a list of the most common fears that people express as they embark on a path toward financial prosperity.

The fear of:

1. ...making a mistake
2. ...the unknown
3. ...losing money
4. ...embarrassment about lack of savings

5. ...underperformance as a result of lack of education/ knowledge
6. ...disappointing the ones we love
7. ...facing potential failure in achieving goals
8. ...admitting lack of understanding the principle of money management to a professional
9. ...feeling inadequate
10. ...screwing it up – for those that have a large amount of money

Fear causes hesitation. Yet fears can be overcome. Sometimes we all need a helping hand to get us over our fears. But so many people find it easier to just hope that things will work out than to proactively face their fears or ask for help. This keeps people from having a solid understanding of their finances.

HOW MY PERSONAL MISSION WAS BORN

Our family had a farm which my dad had started when he was very young. He loved and worked the farm for 30 years. But then, in the early 1980's, when family farms were going under every day, dad lost his beloved farm. This was when Willie Nelson went on his first FarmAid concert tour. While I'm sure the FarmAid Concert helped some farmers, it didn't help us. Not long after losing the farm, dad had a massive stroke, which left my mother essentially widowed and having to care for me and my younger sister. The stroke destroyed dad's ability to speak or communicate in any way. He spent the next 11 years in a nursing home confined to a wheelchair. I was 14 years old. This was a devastating time for our family.

To say we were not in a great financial situation would be a colossal understatement. This was my first real exposure to fear. I saw first-hand how financial distress can significantly impact a strong person (my mother) and make them question their most closely-held beliefs. Due to our extremely limited financial resources, my mother, who had previously been one of the strongest people I knew, developed an intense fear of never having enough money to live life on her terms. This led to a severe level of stress and insecurity.

If you have ever been in a similar situation or known someone who has been, you may relate to the deep feeling of helplessness. I can attest to the fact that it is overwhelming to the point of being so frustrating that it turns to anger. Anger and frustration can manifest the motivation to take positive action, or it can lead to paralysis and despair. In my case, I'm happy to report that the anger and frustration I experienced motivated me to action to overcome my fear. The only question at the time was what action to take.

I was only 14, so I had to rely on what I knew so far. My mother was an educator, so I grew up with her reading books to me, sharing her love and respect for books and education. Seeing knowledge as the only solution I could choose at that time, I determined that the only way I could help alleviate some of the stress from mom was to help her with managing finances. After all, money doesn't know or care how old you are.

I took every business, accounting, and finance class offered at school. My junior year of high school I went to a screening of the movie *Wall Street* with one of my best friends, Dr. Kyle Backstrand (he wasn't a Dr. then). When we walked out of the theater, I turned to him and said, "That's what I'm going to do." He laughed and said, "What? Be Gekko or Bud Fox?" I just said "Yes." I am not sure which one I wanted to be at the time, but the point is that I wanted to be in the financial world.

This led to a very unusual experience. In the movie, there is a scene where Bud Fox (Charlie Sheen) is trying desperately to get into Gordon Gekko's (Michael Douglas) office. He mentions to Gekko's assistant that he has a birthday present for Mr. Gekko. When the assistant asks, "What makes you think it's his birthday?" Fox responds, while showcasing a copy of *Fortune* magazine (with Gekko on the cover) "Well, it's in the Bible! I highly suggest you get him a gift."

As a result of that scene, I have been a subscriber to *Fortune* magazine since I was a junior in high school. Ironically, with my first subscription I received what I consider to be the actual business bible – the 1988 Fortune Money Guide, by Marshall Loeb. Mr. Loeb was the long-time editor of *Fortune* magazine, and his book did a phenomenal job educating me about the basics in my early beginnings down this path.

As I progressed in my studies and learned more and more about the financial world, my mother became more trusting in my judgement and invited me into meetings with financial representatives. One evening, we were meeting with a representative and my mother was being led down the path of his presentation. Finally, he asked if there were any questions. Mom turned to me, and I started asking questions. At the end the man said, "You know more about this than I do." That was a turning point in my life. This man told me that I had a "unique affinity for financial management." He also suggested that perhaps I would want to consider this as a career.

In my senior year of high school, my mother had a Christmas party for some people from work and some old friends. In my father's absence, I was positioned to play host while mom handled the logistics. At the party, there was a doctor who was having a small group discussion about investments. I was able to contribute a comment or two. The doctor looked at me in a shocked manner and asked how I knew that. I said, "It was in *Fortune* magazine." He asked, "You read *Fortune* magazine?" I said "Of course!"

A few weeks after the party he called and asked mom if he could talk to me. We talked about investments, the economy, and more. A few weeks later he called again and asked if we could have a meeting in the evening. He brought a prototype of a machine for dentist offices that we all know now – it cures the fillings in the teeth. That machine was in my home in 1989! The doctor was seeking my opinion about whether he should invest in this machine. That event boosted my confidence and determination greatly!

My freshman year of college, my phone rang, and I was offered the opportunity to go to Chicago and trade an account on the Chicago Board of Options Exchange. While it was a great experience with plenty of stories, it didn't take long for me to decide that I did not want to spend my career as a trader on the floor of the exchange. This was when I learned the difference between being a trader and an investor. The investor approach appealed to me more.

PROSPERITY IS MEANT TO BE ENJOYED

Over the years, mom managed and persevered with what she had to work with and always provided a comfortable, loving home and all the necessities for me and my sister. She grew in her career and her income and built a very respectable nest egg. Yet she didn't feel peaceful, nor did she feel she had 'enough' to enjoy her life. That was a source of great frustration for me, especially as mom approached the end of her career and work life.

To look at where we were when dad had his stroke and where she had arrived was an incredible success story! Yet, there was always the next proverbial carrot out in front of her. She believed that if she could just get that next carrot then everything would be wonderful. This is a fallacy.

After one bad health scare, mom admitted that she was deeply afraid of being disabled and not being able to work. I pressed her as to why she felt that way. She had created her own little horror story about all the things that could, and probably would, go wrong and how many things she would not be able to do. She also voiced concern about being a burden to those she loved. Of course, she was remembering dad's experience too. I'm sure that fed into her ideas and her fears.

We sat down and rationally talked about what would likely happen based on mom's actual financial situation rather than her worst fears. I showed her the exact situation she was in financially. I was able to show her that if she were to leave her job (or was laid off or downsized), she would have the resources to continue to enjoy the lifestyle she was currently enjoying for the rest of her life. She finally understood and her concerns were greatly reduced. It was like a huge weight had been lifted from her shoulders. She finally achieved a sense of peace.

During our discussion, none of mom's finances changed, but her perspective changed and so, in many ways, did her life. She went from being pessimistic and saying, "I'll never be able to retire" to being proud and full of life and vigor at her age and not WANTING to retire. This inner peace was incredibly freeing to her. It gave her a new energy that she was able to pour into her work and her personal life. She was able to confidently spend time with, and money on, her kids, grandkids, and great grandkids without worrying, or feeling guilty about it.

This was not only an epiphany for mom but was a breakthrough for me in understanding my role working with clients. I felt such an inspiring sense of satisfaction when I realized I could eliminate fear and help others acquire and enjoy their financial freedom.

THE POWER OF PERSPECTIVE

The power of perspective changes how we view things and how we react. As I mentioned in mom's story, when she finally realized she could relax because her financial house was in order, the only thing that changed was her perspective.

Gaining perspective is an important part of finding peace and overcoming fear as you embark upon financial planning.

One point I'd like to make about fear is that even the wealthy are fearful, lack proper perspective, and often live like prisoners of their wealth instead of living prosperously. One example of this comes from my earliest days with a client who had tremendous wealth, but when I was getting to know him, I found out that he resented his wealth because he felt like a prisoner to it. Until he allowed himself to trust me with the handling of his wealth instead of him having to oversee everything, he had wealth, but he did not have prosperity. He was miserable.

Author, commentator and ex-priest, Jonathon Morris, says that peace is NOT just a lack of war, true peace is the proper ordering of things. Financial planning principles and processes almost always start with getting your financial house in order. By this I mean you must know where you are and where you want to go. It's much like planning a trip. Think about the first thing you do when you look at a map – you try to find where you are, then find where you want to go. Then you chart out the best path to get there. With GPS it's the same. You put in your current location and where you want to go. The rest is done for you automatically. You just follow the directions.

The journey to financial stability and freedom is a process that can only begin with the first step, which is identifying where you are and where you want to go. We plot out the route for you, which might require adjustments along the way. Most of our clients want to know all the steps in the process from A – Z, but in truth they are only responsible for identifying the 'A' and the 'Z.' The next step is for clients to identify their values so that we can plot out a route that aligns with their deeply-held values.

Perspective in the beginning of a journey is certainly not the same as it is as you get closer to your destination, nor is it the same once you arrive at your desired destination. I love sharing with clients the idea that the longer your perspective, the better things look.

In the beginning, your destination looks so far away, so difficult. Sometimes it's hard to imagine you could ever achieve the prosperity you desire. But with conviction and persistent perseverance you can achieve the fearlessness, the peace, and the prosperity that are the end results of solid financial planning. My family is a testament to the truth of this. My mother persisted, and my career blossomed through helping my mom and so many others.

It is my deepest desire that everyone overcome the fears that may be standing in the way. I wish you the comfort that such peace and prosperity bring. First, define what prosperity means to you. Find someone to help you determine where you want to go. Then step fearlessly onto the path that is sure to lead you to that peaceful and prosperous destination that you desire.

About Cory

As Founder and President/CEO of Alterity Wealth Management, LLC, Cory Neumiller leads a team of nationally recognized experts in each of their specific disciplines with a single purpose in mind…leading clients to achieve and maintain their own version of prosperity.

Starting his career as an accountant in a CPA firm, Cory recognized very early that the career path he had chosen by degree, was not where his passion lay, and therefore he could not excel and succeed to his maximum potential. After being introduced to the investment business through one of the CPA firm partners, he decided to pursue that track.

Having built a successful practice in Northern Minnesota, Cory moved to Minneapolis, MN and was quickly recruited into a management position. He proceeded to spend the next twenty years building sales teams, in education and mentoring of financial advisors, and traveling the world.

Prior to starting his own firm in 2018, Cory served in multiple executive management positions with organizations of all sizes, from small to global, and everywhere in between.

After over 20 years in management, in 2019, Cory reassessed where life was taking him and what was important. He realized that the happiest and most content phase of his career was when he was working directly with clients and seeing first-hand the impact a "do-the-next-right- thing" approach can have on the lives of others.

As an expert in the investment philosophy of the Endowment Model, made famous by David Swenson of the Yale Endowment, Cory created a modified version for the benefit of the average investor. In this spirit, Cory does not have a minimum client size, unlike most financial advisors. He says, "I will help anyone if I can help them…I would not want my Mother refused service because she may happen to be $10,000 below someone's arbitrary minimum. The dollar amount is not important… achieving and maintaining prosperity is."

You may contact Cory at his firm: AlterityWealthManagement.com or on LinkedIn and other social media platforms.

CHAPTER 4

IMPROVISE, ADAPT AND OVERCOME TO ACCOMPLISH YOUR MISSION

BY ZACK VISCOMI

*If you find yourself in a fair fight – You didn't plan
your mission properly.*
~ David Hackworth

It was cold. And when I say it was cold, I mean it was really, really cold. It was so cold that 60% of my body was in a sleeping bag standing on a platform, while my head and upper body were sticking out of the top of a truck. Granted, it probably wasn't less than 42 degrees Fahrenheit, but this was the desert – it wasn't supposed to be this cold. There shouldn't have been frost on the trucks, yet here I was sitting in the turret leading a convoy toward Ramadi and I was shivering.

This particular story begins in early January 2010, and we were well into the coldest months in the Al Anbar Province of Iraq. I was a part of the 6th Motor Transport Battalion, a Reservist Battalion made up of locations across the US. We were the last

Marine Battalion to be in Iraq as the Marine Corps presence was being reduced as part of the withdrawal process initiated by President Obama.

We had already been in country since August and operating across the western half of the country, from Ramadi, Fallujah, and Baghdad out to the Syrian border. I was the lead machine gunner on our convoys and our platoon (First Platoon) was tasked with providing security for third party nationals (truck drivers from neutral countries) and KBR drivers (civilian contract truck drivers from the US). We relieved an M.P. unit if I remember correctly. My MOS, or military occupation, was Motor Transport, yet I didn't drive a truck, MRAP or HUMVEE 'outside the wire' a single day I was deployed. I was a machine gunner and the lead gun truck for 90% of the deployment.

This particular night, we had returned to Ramadi where a government building, which we were at a week before, was hit by two Vehicle-Borne Improvised Explosive Devices (VBIED). Our mission was to provide security on the major roads and allow no one to pass while repairs were made to the defensive structures and barriers around the building.

My truck was parked facing down a major throughway, but there was no traffic at this time of night. It was obvious we were there, but we were in total blackout (no lights). With my NVGs, I could tell that there was small arms fire (SAF) coming in the direction of my truck, seemingly, from an alley on my right. I couldn't make positive ID on where the SAF was coming from, so, I remember yelling through my turret to the sergeant sitting in the passenger seat, "Hey 'sarnt' I think someone is shooting at me."

My sergeant responded, "Did it hit you?"

"No." I replied.

"Well, let me know when it does." he said. And that was the end of the conversation.

I remember shrugging my shoulders in the moment. He had a good point. There was nothing we could do until something actually went down. Thankfully, it never did. However, I have had many years to think back on that instance and reflect on the power of those few words we exchanged that night.

In the moment, his response was comical. In fact, for a long time after, I would retell this moment as a funny story to sum up the entire deployment. However, as I matured and have had the time to think more about this interaction, I realized that there were many fundamental principles at work. Unbeknownst to the sergeant and myself, this short conversation had deeper implications that not only harkened back to our training, but to his experience having been in battle before, and what it means to be on a mission, or rather 'Mission-Driven.' Here are a few of the Principles I learned from that night:

Every plan is a good one – until the first shot is fired.
~ Carl Von Clausewitz

Principle 1: Improvise, Adapt and Overcome

Improvise, Adapt and Overcome is the unofficial slogan of the United States Marine Corps and a fundamental principle to being mission-ready, no matter your circumstance. At Celebrity Branding Agency, we talk about working with 'Mission-Driven CelebrityExperts®' because it is the people who are known for being experts in their field (CelebrityExpert®), not just known, and not just expert, who are able to take their businesses to the next level. However, it is the mission-driven part of that which really makes a difference in an entrepreneur, person, or a professional's ability, to achieve success.

It is easy to think of 'mission-ready' as knowing and executing the plan to perfection. While this is a necessary step in the preparation for and fundamental to the success of many missions, it's the ability of the operator(s) to be well-trained, well-educated, and well-equipped so they are capable of improvising in the face of the inevitable surprises and unexpected turns that arise outside of the predetermined plan. It's their well-rounded knowledge and understanding that allows them to be adaptable to their environment and utilize the resources they have around them to continue and complete the mission.

Improvise: To improvise is the use of one's imagination and instinct to develop a new plan in the wake of an unexpected situation or emergency that renders the original plan irrelevant.

Adapt: To be adaptable is the ability to assess an issue or obstacle in addition to the resources you have available in order to fashion a new solution or a more suitable use of something to fit the current circumstance allowing for further progress.

Shannon Lee in her book, *Be Water, My Friend*, discusses her dad's philosophy about life and martial arts. Her dad, being the one and only Bruce Lee, was a life-long student and spent just as much time training his mind as he did his body. One of his foundational tenets was to be like water – to be fluid, flexible, and ready, but also relaxed. It is this same philosophy that is embodied within this principle to Improvise, Adapt, and Overcome.

She tells a story of a fighter who was being interviewed on TV about how he was going to win the fight. He laid out the exact plan to the reporter in great detail. How he was going to respond to his opponent and in which ways and at what times. He had it all perfectly orchestrated and was ready to execute his well thought-out and practiced plan.

Shannon knew, immediately, he was going to lose the fight,

and, sure enough, he did. Why? We are taught in school and in life that being prepared and having a plan – and executing that plan – is the key to success. Structure and order are instilled in us from the moment we are born. In many ways this is for our own good, and beneficial to our wellbeing as we learn how the world works. But it also puts undue pressure on our ability to achieve from a very young age. 'The Plan' is for us to behave, go to school, get good grades, go to a respectable university, get a job, start a family, have 2.5 children, and retire in Florida.

The reality is that reality always throws us curveballs, and it doesn't matter what 'plan' you have, something is going to disrupt it. You can't plan for something like the COVID-19 pandemic in 2020. It was something that just happened to the world, and changed all of our lives in one way or another. Many good businesses closed, jobs were lost, people were struggling. However, we also saw the improvisation and adaptability of others. New businesses started, the many mission-driven CelebrityExperts® that I work with found new ways to engage with their audience. If they had in-person consultations, they quickly learned how to do them virtually. Some people pivoted directions altogether, but because of their mission to help more people and live the life they wanted, they did not allow this unplanned catastrophe to keep them from continuing toward their objective.

In the case of the aforementioned fighter, the dependence he put on his plan did not allow him to adapt to his opponent, so, he continually tried to force his plan on his current circumstance. It was because of his inability to improvise and adapt that he was not able to overcome. And the same is true in our lives and businesses.

Planning is a crucial step in making sure that you are prepared. But in the words of the 34th President, Dwight D. Eisenhower, "In preparing for battle I have always found that plans are useless, but planning is indispensable."

What do you do when faced with something you did not plan for? How do you respond?

When situations arise, do not be discouraged, you have all you need within to overcome the challenge. Stay focused on your mission and don't be afraid to improvise and adapt so you can overcome.

> *The wise adapt themselves to circumstances as*
> *water molds itself to the pitcher.*
> ~ Chinese Proverb

Principle 2: Give Up Control Without Losing Control

When I told my sergeant what was happening, inside I knew there was nothing I could do. It was completely out of my control because our rules of engagement (ROE) were clear: You must make positive ID before returning fire and I could only respond in like force. In other words, I couldn't just open fire with my truck mounted .50 cal machine gun at someone who was lobbing SAF in my direction.

The truth was I felt out of control, and I wasn't sure what to do. Frankly, I didn't feel like getting shot that night – it was too cold to deal with that. This was not the only time that I felt out of control during this deployment but it is a good example of what it means to give up control without losing it.

There are many studies that have been conducted on both animal and human subjects and many of these studies show that the need for control is innate. However, is control just an illusion? These studies also found that our perceived control is based on our ability to have a choice. We are inclined to choose the route that awards us additional choices, rather than one that does not, even if the result is the same. In many instances, the route that requires more choices also requires the expenditure of more energy, yet this is the path most often taken.

Our instinct is to want control over lives and circumstances. People who want control over their lives are often more driven toward success and usually achieve it. To be mission-driven in life and in business requires some level of control – to make choices that will lead to the outcome you desire, which leads you toward your final objective. We all define success differently, but we all believe that choice is the ticket to get us there.

So, what happens when we feel we do not have a choice? We feel out of control and 'backed into a corner.' When our brain senses us losing our perceived control, we are often kicked into a fight-or-flight response, and this is no place to be making any decisions. You know that feeling in your chest you get that rises in us from the pit of your stomach. It's in these moments that we must reassess where we are and remember, no matter the situation, we always have a choice. Even in moments where we feel there is only one option, the reality is that there is always another. While sitting in that turret, I had a choice. I could remain there focusing on my sector of fire and keeping the people behind me safe; I could also return fire and break the ROE to try and scare off whoever was firing and run the risk of a court martial, but still have my life; I could also have gotten inside the truck, where there was no risk of being shot, but also put the lives of many others at risk.

If we believe that we do not have a choice in any situation (as adults), we make ourselves the victim, and start to blame our circumstances for why we are not able to achieve the goals that we desire. I do not have the time to go into a full psychological breakdown of how and why this affects us negatively, but suffice it to say, that when we are put into situations that we cannot control, but are on a mission, we are making the choice to push forward, despite the rising uncertainty.

In that moment on the truck, I made the choice to remain at my post and ensure the safety of those behind me and in my truck so we could complete the mission we set out to accomplish. If

I would have ducked inside the truck, who knows what would have happened. Probably nothing, but because the mission was more important I gave up control of my safety, without losing control on how that would be accomplished within the context of the mission objective.

As the Chinese proverb stated, water, although it gives up control of its shape to the mold of the container, it does not lose itself in the process. While we may have to bend and flow and give up control in a situation, it does not mean that we lose all control over the outcomes or who we are as a person. We must be willing to conform, like water, but ready to flow free toward our goals once the moment allows it.

It is possible for the same thing both to be and not to be.
~ David Hume

Principle 3: Perception Is Reality, But Doesn't Make You Right

When we are going about our lives and facing different circumstances that disrupt our plans, requiring us to improvise, adapt, and relinquish some control, we must ask ourselves one more question:

Is this really a threat, or is it just a perceived threat?

My sergeant's question "Did it hit you," and subsequent response, "Well, let me know when it does," brings this question to light. Sitting in that turret it seemed like the SAF was a threat or had the potential to become a greater threat. I was taking all my assumptions of what I know about war, about people shooting at me, about how I should or shouldn't respond in this situation and applying those assumptions to my unidentified pseudo-assailant. My inability, on my own, to determine the imminence of this threat hinged on my own assumptions as well as my lack of experience. It wasn't until I said something to my sergeant that it all became clear.

I did not need to respond or do anything about this perceived threat, it's not until it became a real threat that it would require my attention and action. While perception is our reality, it is merely our interpretation of reality. If you are sitting across the table from someone with the number 9 between you, while it is a 9 to you, it is also a 6 to the person on the other side. Who is right? Neither is right, or both are right depending on how you look at it, but if you dig a little deeper, we will have to ask who drew the number and what did they intend it to be? That is the actual reality of that number, despite our perspective on it.

In the end, the choice is always up to you, but don't be afraid to seek out the advice and wisdom of others who have been there before you. Don't be distracted by assumptions and fears and allow them to control you. Give up your control, but don't lose it. Be flexible, improvise, adapt and you will overcome.

Empty your mind, be formless, shapeless, like water
Put water into a cup, it becomes the cup
Put water into a teapot, it becomes the teapot
Water can flow or creep, drip, or crash
Be water my friend.
~ Bruce Lee

About Zack

For over 20 years, Zack Viscomi has shown repeated success in leadership as well as business development, branding,operations, and sales. Zack has worked with hundreds of entrepreneurs and professionals all around the world in the development of their CoreStory as well as teaching the powerof The Business Trifecta®, the proven system behind business growth, and providing the tools needed to live a life of Joyful Impact and Significance.

Zack is the President of Celebrity Branding Agency and Integrator of DNA Media. He is a Best-Selling Author and has been featured in *USA Today.* He has also been seen on *ABC, NBC, CBS,* and *Fox* affiliates around the country. As an Ambassador for the Global Entrepreneurship Initiative at Carnegie Hall, he presented on stage about the importance of story for businesses and how we all have a story to share.

Whether it's developing new processes, hiring, training, and implementing technology to help a service and repair company post profitable quarters after continually experiencing net losses, or developing a system for the accounting department to decrease another company's receivables by over 70%, Zack is passionate about helping people succeed, while becoming the best versions of themselves.

Zack also enjoys mountain biking and spending time with his wife, Alli, and their three children, Scout, Aries, and Poppy – not to forget their two dogs: a boxer/ridgeback/pitbull mix named Miley, and a mini-pug named Mona.

Learn more at:
- ZackViscomi.com
- Celebritybrandingagency.com

CHAPTER 5

SHAKEN BUT NEVER BROKEN

BY DR. ASMAIT YOHANNES

The gift of life is magical, mysterious, challenging, exciting and can be extraordinary when you know how to make use of your mind, emotions, your God-given talents and, when you truly understand that you are a gift of God. I came into this world in Ethiopia from two Eritrean parents in eastern Africa through my amazing mother who, along with my grandmother, raised me and taught me how to love and respect myself, to discover my talents and to live MY LIFE according to my heart, not according to someone else's ideas or opinions.

But, let me go back to the time when I was still in my mother's womb. While my mother was pregnant with me, her father, my maternal grandfather had a vision. He told my mother he saw very clearly that she was going to give birth to a girl who would be strong and talented, and powerful. This child, my grandfather told my mother, would leave an important legacy at the end of her life. My grandfather also suggested that my mother should name me Asmait, which in the native language in Eritrea means legacy.

My grandfather passed on when I was just three months old, so

71

I never knew him. Yet, here I am, living as he envisioned with the name he suggested. It seems I came into life with a very specific and important mission.

As a woman of color born in East Africa and educated in a school system where lessons were taught in British English, I learned that the way my mother and grandmother nurtured and raised me was quite special. I also discovered the work of Maya Angelou at a young age, at which point she became one of my main role models along with my mother and grandmother. With her words, Maya carved out a path for women of color to follow throughout the ages and showed us that our dreams are guides.

Her poem, *And Still I Rise*, provides a beacon of light that continues to serve me on my journey to fulfilling my life's mission. I share portions of the poem throughout, and in its completion at the end of this chapter for those who may not know it, and to highlight how it has served and continues to inspire me.

NEVER DEVIATE FROM THE TRUTH
OF YOUR DREAMS

"Just like moons and like suns,
With the certainty of tides,
Just like hopes springing high,
Still I'll rise."

If you can imagine the most meaningful life, you can live it. If you stay true to your dreams, they will come to pass. By merely living with a pure mind, leading with excellence, and making your life a message for others to take guidance from, you will be an inspiration for the good of all. This is how I live and is the reason why I am so often asked, "What is the secret behind the successful, joyful, and calm life you're living?"

The purpose of life is an eternal question that has fascinated mankind since the beginning of human existence. Without meaning, it is very easy to wander pointlessly through life instead of following your life's North Star. Without purpose, it is extremely easy to squander time rather than wake up each morning with an unquenchable thirst for attaining your mission. Without purpose, one certainly may achieve extraordinary success, yet still feel as if life is meaningless.

Finding one's purpose in life is integral to living a life that becomes mission-driven. A purpose-filled life inspires and motivates not only oneself but others. When you discover your purpose, you will begin to feel good about who you are, what you stand for, and where you are heading. When you find out your life's purpose, inner peace replaces the need to seek approval from anyone. And people will begin to sense a new you – someone who is cheerful, motivated as well as self-assured, a person on a mission. People will start to say that there is something extraordinary about you.

REMAIN STRONG IN THE FACE OF CHALLENGING TIMES

"Did you want to see me broken?
Bowed head and lowered eyes?
Shoulders falling down like teardrops,
Weakened by my soulful cries?"

From a very young age I knew I wanted to have my own business. I wanted to be a Founder/Chief Executive Officer (CEO) and to be in a position where I could lead, teach, and inspire others. I learned that not everyone receives the kind of positive encouragement my mother and grandmother provided. Knowing this is one of the main reasons that helping others discover meaning and live with purpose fills me every day.

I arrived in America with one mission and goal – to pursue the American dream. My dreams included becoming very well educated in every area that would serve a Founder/Chief Executive Officer of a thriving company. My interest in helping others motivated me toward the healing profession. I earned a nursing degree, and continued into health management and public health, and I was able to get employment in a hospital. I worked during the day and went to school at night to pursue my higher education. With this background I knew I would be able to take bigger steps toward my goal of becoming the Founder/ CEO of my own company.

With my collective business knowledge, fiscal expertise, and strong leadership, I landed an executive post as Vice-Chair in the corporate health care sector. Believe me, I had many challenges working with medical doctors (surgeons) who made assumptions about my abilities based on the color of my skin and also that I was a woman. I came face-to-face with the daily microaggressions people of color endure, and especially women of color in the workplace. An assumption is made, often by men, though not exclusively by men, that "Blacks and Hispanics are deviant or professionally less ambitious."

The Status of Women of Color in the Workplace 2021 report also states, "Microaggressions that single out Blacks and Hispanics based on assumptions made about their academic success or the way they articulate triggers the notion that Blacks and Hispanics are not an intellectual group, and the notion that those who have succeeded in this area are the exception or out of their jurisdiction. Similarly, stereotypes paint Asian-Americans as an academically successful group. These same stereotypes construe them as a well-behaved demographic seldom sought out for leadership. These stereotypes obstruct the full potential of women of color at work." [1]

I came face to face with the mistaken notion that I was 'out of my jurisdiction' when working with surgeons whose schedules I had authority to change if necessary. Whenever my authority and worth came into question by professionals who were not accustomed to being challenged in any way, especially not by

1.https://www.womenofcolorintheworkplace.com/_files/ugd/f9faf1_2a2dd 0cf83ba449ab25fc0cb25c477bd.pdf

a woman of color, I stood my ground. I called on the love and strength my family cultivated in me and repeated my mantra: "You can shake me, but you can never break me." I knew that no one was coming to my rescue, no one else was going to come to stand up and fight for me. I didn't need anyone to come to my rescue. I am my own savior. This is what I learned from the two strong women who raised me and from Maya Angelou.

This is the message I share with all the beautiful women who come to hear me speak, those who listen to my podcast, and those with whom I interact in my business. I emphasize that we each have the God-given power to use our faith, integrity, and strength to help others who knowingly or unknowingly repress us, then awaken to their mistaken behavior.

EMBRACE REJECTION, LEARN TO LOVE IT AND SEE WHERE IT CAN TAKE YOU

"You may write me down in history
With your bitter, twisted lies,
You may trod me in the very dirt
But still, like dust, I'll rise."

I have achieved my dream of being the Founder/CEO of my own company, and my mission continues. I feel strong, like a black diamond. I have overcome every challenge placed in my path as other women of color have for centuries. I know there is nothing that life can place in my path that I could not overcome with faith. If you face rejection, whether it be in your professional or personal life, it may shake you up, but it cannot break you unless you let it. That phrase, which is the title I've chosen for this chapter, is my mantra.

Whenever I am faced with challenges of any kind, especially in the form of rejection due to discrimination, I am bolstered by my mantra. I know that simply by shifting my understanding about the one who seems to be rejecting me and shine my love upon whatever I am faced with, it will reveal something wonderful either in the way of greater learning or even more exciting opportunities. Very often a new door opens to something greater than I could have imagined.

My mother and grandmother instilled in me the power of strong women and four core pearls of wisdoms. They are:

1. Bounce back from any fall out
2. Adore my Self and stay true to who I aspire to be
3. Know when to eliminate naysayers
4. Become notable for my greatness in the world.

When motivated by reasons that are nourishing, altruistic, and grounded in truth, our motivation to continue to strive for our dreams grows stronger.

LEARN TO LEAD BY FOLLOWING YOUR DREAMS

Nature is consistent. When we look to nature, as Maya Angelou did in her beautiful tribute to all women, we can feel the unending flow of life, just like the forces that hold the sun and moon in the sky and the forces that create the rhythmic tides. We are part of nature. The same forces flow in our veins.

I lead by following my dreams and I hope you will do the same. Our dreams derive from our deepest nature, and they will lead us to our mission. We have the power to persist in our dreams that call us toward them and seem to nudge us onward from behind. As we continue to pursue our dreams, our inner beauty also shines brighter. Today, as a Certified Business Consultant, a law school student, and the Founder/CEO of my own skincare and beauty company, my mission now includes consulting with women who are starting their own businesses, as well as continually drawing out and balancing their inner and outer beauty. I love to remind women that as expressions of life itself, they deserve to feel their beauty, to see it shine back at them when they look into a mirror.

I see myself and every woman of color like beautiful, strong, black diamonds. Black diamonds are thought to symbolize purity, love, fidelity, and eternity. They are also considered to be a symbol of power, charisma, certainty, and passion.

As a mission driven businesswoman, I am encouraged by the incredible progress I see in the lives of so many women. While there is always more progress to be made if each of us finds our purpose and is true to our life's mission, we will continue to see greater and greater achievements by women in every sector of society. I leave you with the amazing, powerful words of Maya Angelou. May you take them to heart and give them the power to stand your ground and perhaps even adopt my personal mantra:

You can shake me, but you can never break me.

And Still I Rise
By Maya Angelou

You may write me down in history
With your bitter, twisted lies,
You may tread me in the very dirt
But still, like dust, I'll rise.

Does my sassiness upset you?
Why are you beset with gloom?
'Cause I walk like I've got oil wells
Pumping in my living room.

Just like moons and like suns,
With the certainty of tides,
Just like hopes springing high,
Still I'll rise.

Did you want to see me broken?
Bowed head and lowered eyes?
Shoulders falling down like teardrops,
Weakened by my soulful cries?

Does my haughtiness offend you?
Don't you take it awful hard
'Cause I laugh like I've got gold mines
Diggin' in my own backyard.

You may shoot me with your words,
You may cut me with your eyes,
You may kill me with your hatefulness,
But still, like air, I'll rise.

Does my sexiness upset you?
Does it come as a surprise
That I dance like I've got diamonds
At the meeting of my thighs?

Out of the huts of history's shame
I rise
Up from a past that's rooted in pain
I rise
I'm a black ocean, leaping and wide,
Welling and swelling I bear in the tide.

Leaving behind nights of terror and fear
I rise
Into a daybreak that's wondrously clear
I rise
Bringing the gifts that my ancestors gave,
I am the dream and the hope of the slave.
I rise
I rise
I rise

About Dr. Asmait

An accomplished leader and dynamic international speaker and award-winning author, Dr. Asmait Yohannes overcame countless challenges and obstacles in pursuit of her lifelong dream of becoming a Founder/CEO. Her path to entrepreneurial freedom began when she successfully transitioned from a career in nursing to an executive post as a vice-chair in corporate health care, where she rose through the ranks in a highly competitive, male-dominated environment. Today, Asmait brings that collective business knowledge, fiscal expertise, and leadership to her role as founder and CEO of her own company, Asmait Skin Care and Design, LLC.

Asmait credits her perseverance and success to the remarkable resilience of her mother and grandmother who taught her to bounce back from every fallout in life, to always adore herself and stay true to who she aspires to be, to know when to eliminate naysayers, and to be notable for her greatness in the world.

As a woman entrepreneur, Asmait's primary goal and passion are to help bring out the natural beauty in every woman, and to provide empowerment and inspiration to women worldwide by sharing the timeless pearls of wisdom of her ancestors. Asmait has been seen on *FOX, NBC* & *CBS* news.

In gratitude to the female mentors and role models who helped her evolve into the woman she is today, Asmait is deeply committed to giving back and inspiring other women to courageously follow their dreams. She generously funds Asmait Yohannes Scholarships for young women attending Nightingale Nursing School in Uganda. She also hosts an inspirational podcast, *Inner Beauty*, where she spotlights successful women entrepreneurs.

CHAPTER 6

PASSION DRIVES MISSION
CHOOSING THE MOMENT TO
CHANGE YOUR LIFE

BY FUNK ROBERTS

A pivotal moment describes a time in life that provides impetus and clarity through which opportunity for change appears. Inaccurate perceptions can often lead to misinformed decision making. Simply put, garbage in equals garbage out. My moment of clarity came after countless attempts to live in a version of my manhood that was fed by stereotypes and inflated generalizations about what it means to be a man. This lifestyle caught up to me and left me in darkness.

As a professional athlete, I was dedicated to maintaining good health through diet and exercise. Even beyond the necessity of keeping my body primed for the demands of professional sports, I had a passion for fitness. When the age of YouTube was born, I had an outlet to share my passion with others. I was working hard, but hardly seeing any results. One day, I eventually reached my breaking point. It did not matter that my efforts were consistent. My commitment to a healthy lifestyle did not yield a physicality matching the effort I was exerting. I felt like a fraud. Promoting health and wellness, yet I was not achieving the health and wellness results I wanted. Pair these undesirable results with diminished confidence, decreasing sex-drive, a relationship ending, and dissatisfaction in many aspects of my life. The coping mechanisms I chose landed me in patterns of excessive partying and false bravado. Here I was, struggling to see my purpose and disconnected from my passion; it was no surprise that I felt lost in my journey.

Searching for answers, I made an appointment with my doctor. I learned my testosterone levels were plummeting, and suddenly, every symptom I was battling had a cause I could name. Did it make sense at first? No. Did I know I had a new challenge ahead of me? Yes. I was given a new task; redefine what 'healthy' meant for me. I had no desire to rely on traditional treatment measures to regulate my testosterone levels. That was a hard pass for me, and instead, I searched high and low for more holistic approaches. No matter where I looked, all I found was a gap. There was no one helping men like me, so I did it for myself.

I found a path out of my darkness. I changed what I was eating and how I was exercising. I started seeing the results that I had been longing to achieve. My life pivoted in a powerful way. I was excelling in my career, focused on my passion, and rejuvenated in my personal life. Until I was caught by a rare and terrifying disease. A total mystery of unexplained symptoms. One by one they started to rule out any and every possibility. Finally, the doctors found that my lungs were being crushed by a disease called cryptogenic organizing pneumonia (COP). My treatment was corticosteroids. While targeted to resolve the COP, this treatment was an overt attack on my body.

Like a time-machine, I was forced back to that pivotal moment in my life. I knew the only answer was to get my habits back in order. I started eating a diet that promoted healing in my body, restoring my testosterone and overall well-being. I got back to my regimen of exercise and training. A customized plan that promoted better health for my body and age. But then, I started to think about the other men like me – over 40 and struggling to breakthrough whatever might be blocking them from their goals. Add to that, the perception that there is no help or community available to them and they are not sure where to start. I reflected on my catalyst to choose change. Misconceptions plagued my outlook on life, and I was hyper-focused on continuing rituals and behaviors that were reliable for only one thing, not returning the results I needed. However, I didn't know what else to try. I needed support that was meant for me and my specific challenges, but none existed.

YOUR PASSION WILL DRIVE YOUR MISSION

Finding your passion will not be linear. There will be days when your passion is pulsing through your veins and your motivation has no limits. Other days, your passion will seem like a distant thought, barely formed and waning. It is your passion, however, that will be the flame along your journey. My journey of overcoming my own challenges helped me identify that my purpose is fulfilled through helping others. Combining my passion for fitness with my purpose to help others, I found a mission to develop a program helping men over 40 grab the reins on their life. A healthy body supports a healthy life, so that's where I decided to start:

1. Start with yourself: The power to change and create impact comes from within. Even when all the resources and support can be collected like firewood, the fire has to first be started by you. Think about what you love. Think about what reveals itself in your daily thoughts. What topics are you always discussing? What inspires you to keep learning? This is where passion is born.
2. Try Something: Once you've identified that thing (or several things), try it out. Learn more, talk with others, get involved. This is how a passion is nurtured. Align your habits and choices to support this emerging interest.

Commit yourself to this practice and narrow the focus as you have more information.

3. <u>Make it Permanent:</u> It's going to take time and intention and that's why you have to prioritize your passion. Everything else follows when you let your passion lead. This means practicing every day, always including your passion on your to-do list, and remaining committed even when it isn't easy. Make a plan and stick to that plan.

COMMUNITY MAKES A DIFFERENCE

When I set out after this new mission to help men like me, I was not considering what would probably become the most impactful and inspiring element of the program, the brotherhood. On days when you are struggling, the Alpha Brotherhood is there for you. When that voice in your head is trying to convince you to give up, the Alpha Brotherhood is cheering you on and rooting for your success. When the world is pushing their views of what it means to be a man, the Alpha Brotherhood lets you find strength through vulnerability.

You have to build the community you want to surround you. Many of us have heard the saying, 'You are the company you keep.' When we surround ourselves with those that have similar goals and desires, it contributes to a supportive environment. Let's discuss the science behind human connection. An article from *Yale Medicine Magazine* reads:

> *Human survival has depended on sharing information and working alongside others within social groups. Yet, paradoxically, loneliness can reinforce isolation by triggering hypervigilance and eroding self-image. The way out, said [Vivek] Murthy, is to help others.*

Many studies have been conducted to understand the impact of human connection and, in comparison, isolation and solitude. It has been concluded that the benefits of feeling connected to others can include high self-esteem, a reduction in anxiety and depression, and improved emotion regulation skills. I am moved every time that I login to the Over 40 Alpha Facebook group. Men have reconnected with themselves, and in turn, contribute to building a community of support and love. We share our successes, we rally around those seeking support, and we encourage and coach each other to be outstanding men, husbands, fathers, sons, and friends.

RESULTS MOTIVATE, RESULTS INNOVATE

One of the first things you might notice when looking through the Over 40 Alpha Program is the celebration of results achieved. Results reaffirm the hard work and dedication you have committed to living your mission. Results can also lead to course correction and improvements. Even better, results can help inspire innovation. When I want to know what my next move is, I look to my results to inform me on what's working and what needs to change. Results motivate me when I'm struggling to stay consistent. They act as a reminder of what can be achieved. Results keep me focused on my mission.

However, it's important to ensure results are being considered both quantitatively and qualitatively. Numbers without context cannot tell a story, and stories are needed to inspire. Data-driven decision making may be the hottest new trend, and for good reason. However, there is a misconception that data alone can arm you with insights and analysis that support prescriptive action plans. Another half-truth that could lead you down the wrong path is not adjusting what is actually being measured for results. As you continue to change, evolve, and innovate on your journey, it will become best practice to revisit the results you have set as targets. You can choose to move the goalposts when appropriate. Setting an evolved goal that takes into consideration the learnings you've gained and the new information and/or perspectives you have, will only further support your pursuit to live in your mission.

Your pivotal moment might be right around the corner. Maybe you find yourself in the midst of that moment right now. You have the power to put a plan in motion today by prioritizing your passion. Align every action to find and live out your purpose. I have found that my purpose is helping other men create a healthy body and mind, supporting them as they renew their commitment to themselves.

For anyone out there starting on this journey, the lessons I've learned along the way are simple and straightforward:

1. ***Your Passion Will Drive Your Mission:*** Find it. Nurture It. Prioritize It.
2. ***Community Makes a Difference:*** Create a community that supports, encourages, and promotes the growth and success you are seeking; and in return, a community that benefits from your engagement, creating a mutually beneficial ecosystem.
3. ***Results Motivate, Results Innovate:*** Whether you're needing a boost to stay the course, or searching for an opportunity to improve and evolve, results will guide you.

About Funk

Funk Roberts is the President and Creator of Funk Roberts Fitness Inc, Funk Supplements and Over 40 Alpha Brotherhood. As a former Professional Beach Volleyball player and Muay Thai fighter, Funk knows how to train at the highest levels.

Now he is a leading Fitness Expert around the world and the creator of the Over 40 Alpha Brotherhood for Men Over 40, which is a monthly membership program with over 14,000 members (growing everyday), dedicated to helping men over 40, 50 and 60 naturally increase their testosterone levels while transforming health, fitness, weight loss, business and life through new monthly workouts, programs, nutrition info, mindset, supplementation, sleep strategies, recovery routines, exclusive products, motivation, master classes, community and more.

Funk is an online Fitness Entrepreneur who successfully runs two 7-figure businesses and is a recent recipient of the 2-Comma Club Award through Clickfunnels, which is for generating $1 million dollars in one year using one funnel. He was also just awarded the prestigious Presenter of the Year Award from CanFitPro for 2022.

Funk's passion has also allowed him to create National Testosterone Awareness Day each November 17th and is focused on the primary male hormone for men.

Funk is also a Certified Master Metabolic Trainer, Certified MMA Conditioning Coach (MMACA)-NESTA, Certified Fitness Nutrition Coach, Core Conditioning Specialist-NESTA, Kettlebell Training Specialist, Pain-Free Performance Specialist and Mindset Coach.

He has partnered with NESTA (National Exercise and Sports Trainers Association) to create and launch his Metabolic Conditioning Coach Certification Course, which will teach and certify Personal/Bootcamp Trainers and Coaches using HIIT and metabolic training. This course has become the most popular certification in the NESTA Library.

Funk is a two-time Amazon #1 Best Selling Author for *Over 40 Shred* and *Rapid Body Makeover*, and has appeared as a Fitness and Celebrity Expert on

ABC, NBC, CBS, and FOX TV affiliates and has been featured in *GQ Magazine, Muscle & Fitness, Train Fitness Magazine, Inside Fitness Magazine, Men's Journal, Status Magazine, Yahoo Health, Healthline*, along with many others.

He is driven to helping one million men over the age of 40 completely transform their lives and regain their manhood by 2025 – by educating and empowering men on the importance of health and fitness for their lives, their wives, their kids, their families, and the community around them.

Funk has a following of 710,000 subscribers on *YouTube* along with 120,000 email subscribers and over one million followers on Facebook in which he communicates on a daily to weekly basis.

At 53 years old, Funk is happily married with two older sons, with a passion to traveling the world, training *muay thai* in Thailand, working with the UFC, hanging online with his Over 40 Alpha's and spending quality time with his family.

To Learn more please visit:
- www.over40alpha.com

CHAPTER 7

FROM CHAOS TO PURPOSE TO MISSION

BY MICHAEL MILLER, CFP®

When I think about the essence of the word 'mission', my mind immediately moves to the word 'purpose'. Though used interchangeably, the word 'purpose' has a slightly different context for me. It's more personal, and the word provided strong motivation in my life long before I became truly mission-motivated. In my mind, mission has a broader meaning, less personal, and has both religious and military connotations. This broader sense of influencing others did not come into my life until later in my story.

If you are holding this book in your hands, you are likely looking for meaning in some aspect of your life. Please trust and know that wherever you are, whatever challenges you are facing, you are right where you are meant to be. Despite many challenges, as I look back on the roads I've travelled, and as I look forward to those yet unknown adventures, I am confident that opportunities and inspiration are ever present for every single person – no matter how bleak or confusing current circumstances may appear. My early life can only be considered bleak and challenging, yet, as you will see, every good thing I subsequently experienced and continue to experience, was shaped and born by my response to the opportunities embedded in each challenge. Until I was 16 years old, I had no sense of purpose. My life seemed meaningless. But in my 16th year, my purpose came into being. Here's how it happened.

THE BIRTH OF MY PURPOSE

In deep, dark, dead of night I was awakened by thunder, lightning, torrential rain, and my mom and sister squeezing into my two-man pup tent. I felt disoriented and confused. The rain had collapsed their tent and moments later did the same to mine. The three of us untangled ourselves and crawled out of the soggy collapsed tent. We ran through the downpour to the car. There we sat through the night, in the KOA campground, shivering in wet clothes. I was 16, and we were homeless.

That night, the seeds of purpose and success were simultaneously sparked and rooted firmly in my heart and soul. I vowed I would be wealthy and never suffer lack and poverty as an adult, nor would I allow this kind of experience to happen to my children. In that very moment, my life took on powerful new meaning. Prior to this experience, I had no sense of direction, no sense of meaning in life. But that night, I stepped onto a path from which I have never veered. When I look back and remember the cold I felt and the sadness of that night which gave birth to an intense burning desire and determination to change my life. I am filled with gratitude for that experience. Without it, I would not be who I am today.

PURPOSE MOTIVATED TO MISSION DRIVEN

For I know the plans I have for you, declares the Lord,
plans to prosper you and not to harm you,
plans to give you hope and a future.
~ Jeremiah 29:11 (NIV)

Mom, sis, and I lived in pup tents at a KOA campground in Tampa, Florida for six months before we were able to get into government housing. By then, I knew without a doubt that I wanted to work in the financial business. My desire to understand how to manage money motivated me to read and study everything I could get my hands on. I learned about compound interest and was hooked. I also knew I wanted to go to college but realized there was no money for college, nor was I scholarship material. So, after graduation, I enlisted in the army. At least I knew that when I got out – if I got out alive – college would be paid for.

I served in the 82nd Airborne Division of the Army, where, as a paratrooper I jumped out of perfectly good airplanes, flown and crewed by the great men and women of the Air Force.

As I mentioned, no one was offering me scholarships in high school. I struggled with dyslexia as a child, which made me realize I had to work harder than anyone else. While most people think dyslexia is a bad thing, it inspired me to work harder to achieve.

RIGHT PLACE RIGHT TIME

In the army, I learned not only about mission and serving a greater good, but also about how important it is to help people find what they are good at, in other words, their right place. Initially, the army tried to train me to be a linguist. I spent nearly half a year in training and was terrible and terrified the entire time. To say I failed miserably is an understatement. Even though I tried hard, I was so bad that the army wasn't sure what to do with me. After further testing, they decided to send me for training as an intelligence analyst instead.

After training, I arrived at my permanent duty station as an intelligence analyst for the 313th Military Intelligence Battalion, 82nd Airborne Division at Fort Bragg, North Carolina. Shortly after arriving to my unit, the 18th Airborne Corp called over and asked my commander if they could spare an extra 'analyst' to work in their 'SCIF' which was where intelligence data was gathered, collected, and analyzed in a great big vault. For some reason, my commanding office decided to send me. I believe it was because I was new, and they could spare me at the time. It was all so new to me. During some down time, I was given some coded messages in Spanish to look at, and I didn't speak a word of that language. There was only one code breaker on Fort Bragg at the time and she was busy running the cell. She told me not to worry about cracking the code as there were some very powerful computers at NSA working on them and I had not been trained to break code. I took that as a challenge.

At the end of a very frustrating day of fruitless efforts, I had a dream in which I saw newspaper strips going in different directions. After waking up and wondering what that was all about, I went in to work and, almost immediately started noticing repeating patterns and started writing out a cypher key and worked that into the messages that lay before me. Much to my amazement, within an hour, what I discovered, when translated into English, made sense to everyone I was working with. I was told with urgency to pick up the red phone which went directly to NSA and share the coded messages with them as well as my cypher key since their computers were unable to crack the code. Shortly after, thinking I was finished, I was told I would have to brief the Commanding General of the 82nd Airborne Division on my findings.

I had to brief the General! Me! A low ranking private, recent linguist reject newbie soldier, now was going to brief the GENERAL on the code I broke and how I did it! Holy Cow! I had never briefed anyone, much less my Commanding General. I was extremely nervous as Power Point was also new to me.

At the suggestion of the intelligence cell leader, I drove home to grab lunch and calm my nerves. As I was driving back to the

SCIF, my Bronco got stuck in deep mud from a rainstorm the night before. The security detail, seeing what was unfolding, came out to help me get unstuck. As I was pushing on the Bronco, the wheels spun mud all over my freshly-pressed uniform and spit-shined boots. I had no time to clean up before the General and his entourage arrived. I was now more nervous than ever. What would the General say about my appearance? Was I in trouble now?

When I walked into the briefing room, filled with high-ranking officers, to my amazement no one mentioned my mud-splattered clothes. They only had an interest in what I had discovered. Everyone in the room seemed impressed with what I had found and how I had found it.

Upon my report to the General, Operation Golden Pheasant was launched in Honduras. This was a defining moment, as defining as that shivering night in the car with my mom and sister had been. I discovered that I am gifted with pattern recognition – a gift I didn't know I had – and my career as an Intelligence Analyst in the 82nd Airborne Division of the Army was launched. I received my first medal and commendation for my work and then had the honor of being one of the select few who ever get to attend code school. It was the first time I felt a true sense of worth. I suddenly realized I had something of value to contribute to the world.

Well done, good and faithful servant! You have been faithful with a few things. I will put you in charge of many things. Come and share your master's happiness!
~ Matthew 25:23

After getting out of the military, I went to college on the GI Bill. I worked and studied hard and was the valedictorian of my graduating class. My wife and I met soon after I went into the army, and we had our daughter within the first year of our marriage, so my motivation to succeed grew stronger.

My understanding of the effect my actions have on the lives of others also grew stronger. Upon graduating I secured a job at Fidelity. After a few years of working my way up the ladder, I earned the highly sought-after Certified Financial Planner (CFP®) designation.

More doors and opportunities opened up for me in the financial services industry. Eventually I was managing over $1 Billion in accounts for thousands of key decision makers and high net worth accounts across nine different states. I really thought I had life all figured out! I was making good money and I had a beautiful family. I built up my financial resources and felt comfortable. Yet I also felt a growing discomfort within.

It didn't take long to figure out that most of the financial industry is built on selling their products. My job wasn't to help others first, but to help the company grow bigger first. I couldn't continue living with the conflicts of interest that came with a broken financial system. This was not what I wanted my life to be about. My desire to help others understand how to manage money and how to achieve their dreams and goals came to the foreground once again. I could not ignore the call. I knew something was missing and I was determined to find out what that something was.

THE IDOLATRY OF MONEY DOES NOT BRING PEACE

Even though I was building up my financial reserves, I always felt I didn't have enough. I kept hearing myself say, "If I only had more money..." Then I started going to church. I had not been raised in any religion. I rarely thought about God until I went to church. This is where I found a peace I didn't have before. It was after this that I stepped out on faith in early 2007, left a high paying six-figure job with benefits to start Miller Premier Investment Planning, LLC.

I continued attending bible study classes and wanted to understand God more deeply. After a bible study one evening, I had another vivid and seemingly prophetic dream that had a dramatic effect on me and how I conducted my life from that moment forward and even to this day. The dream showed me that the only permanent thing in life is our relationships with others and our relationship with God. I began incorporating this philosophy not only in my business practice, but in my personal life. I share this God-given dream and its powerful message every chance I get.

That same verse quoted from the previous page from Matthew 25:23 is the fuel that now drives my mission in life:

Well done, good and faithful servant! You have been faithful with a few things. I will put you in charge of many things. Come and share your master's happiness!

I love the message. While many people think this parable only speaks about money, I believe it speaks to all the gifts God has given each of us in terms of our time, talents, and treasures.

I am now confident in the ways that my God-given talents and skills, learned through hard work and dedication, contribute to the well-being of others. Through my Christian-based financial planning firm, which is not tied to any Wall Street firms, insurance companies or other products, I now help my clients manage their resources, not just through their investments, but through also helping them discover why money is important to them. It's never just about the money, which is simply a tool. It's about what they want to do and how they want to contribute to the greater good.

THE VALUE OF CONTINGENCY PLANNING IN MONEY MANAGEMENT

The military taught me contingency planning. I had no idea that it would become integral in my financial planning business. Contingency planning is a process used in battle testing. Every potential situation and outcome one's actions might result in, is considered, and planned for. We consider what could go wrong and how we will deal with it before any action is ever taken. This kind of planning is so important when you are involved in pursuits that impact the lives of others. You must consider every single aspect of what could or might go wrong and know how you would address every circumstance should it occur. In other words, nothing is left to chance.

I use the contingency planning process when working with my clients. My mission is to manage each of my client's money in the most responsible way according to their very individual and specific needs, goals, and life circumstances. When planning for retirement, the biggest fear most people have is running out of money before they die. I employ Monte Carlo simulation, a class of computational algorithms that rely on repeated random sampling to obtain numerical results. Commonly used in particle physics, biochemistry, and engineering, I find it extremely useful in computing the probability of success in investing. The simulation goes through roughly 10,000 different iterations of what could happen involving small company stocks, large company stocks, value stocks, growth stocks, etc. and I make sure that the probability of success is always above 80%, never lower. The great thing is that I get to help my clients multiply their means to accomplish their meaning in life.

THE EVOLUTION FROM CHAOS TO PURPOSE TO MISSION DRIVEN

That cold, dark night when I was drenched and shivering in the car with my mom and sister seems so far away yet remains prominently etched in my memory. Since that unforgettable night, my journey has taken me from homeless to hopeful, and ultimately to being helpful. The relationships forged along the way are what mean the most to me. The richness of the human spirit forever inspires me. The stories I've been privileged to hear come from clients that range from those who start with very few resources to those who come to me already blessed with prosperity. My mission is to help each client make the most of their financial resources without being taken advantage of in any way. I have had experiences with clients who were being needlessly charged as much as $80,000 in annual fees when they could have been reinvesting that sum to their advantage.

My 16-year-old imagination could not have envisioned the glorious and unexpected turns my life has taken. A spark of determination and sustained motivation was all that was needed. From the intensely personal purpose, my life drew me to serve the greater good. For that I am eternally grateful. I pray that whatever road you are on that you are traversing it with purpose, meaning and mission. May you find inspiration in every event and prosperity around every corner.

About Michael

A Five Star Award-Winning Wealth Manager, Michael Miller, CFP®, provides tax efficient investment advisory and portfolio management services to top business owners and thought leaders around the world.

Recognized as a leading expert on retirement planning and wealth management, Michael has authored and consulted on numerous publications appearing in such places as *The Wall Street Journal, U.S. News & World Report, Investor's Business Daily, Miami Herald, Texas Monthly,* and *Dallas Morning News.* Michael has served as a subject matter expert for the Certified Financial Planner Board of Standards, Inc. in Washington D.C. and has been a featured speaker to audiences nationwide on the topics of investment and retirement planning. He has had the honor of speaking before the brave men and women at conferences such as the International Association of Fire Fighters, the Fraternal Order of Police, and the Texas Association of Counties' Annual Judges and Commissioners Conferences to teach them how to better prepare for a fulfilling retirement. Michael has also appeared on *Wall Street Today* where he shared how he helps clients bridge the gap between their God-given means and their God-given meaning.

In 2007, at the age of 36, he founded Miller Premier Investment Planning, LLC as an independent, fee-only, fiduciary firm after having managed over $1 Billion in client retirement accounts over a nine-state area for the non-profit ICMA-RC. Prior to that he was the Texas State Director for Nationwide Retirement Solutions where he oversaw the development and servicing of city and county government retirement plans. Michael earned the highly sought after CFP® designation while working for Fidelity Investments in 1999 where he worked with high net-worth clients and was a fixed income specialist for his branch.

Michael was the valedictorian of his graduating class at Fayetteville State University where he earned his degree in Business Administration with a concentration in Banking and Finance. Prior to that he served as a Sergeant in the Army's 82nd Airborne Division where he received numerous medals as an intelligence analyst, team leader, paratrooper, and codebreaker. He is a Gulf War Veteran.

Michael is a member of the National Association of Personal Financial Advisors and the Financial Planning Association. He proudly serves his community and country as a volunteer where he speaks on financial planning topics to community centers, church groups, and schools. He also gives back to his profession as a scholarship review panelist for future generations of up and coming financial planners. As someone who never forgets what it was like to be homeless, Michael also selflessly and joyfully pours his God-given resources of time, talent, and money into his mission of giving joy, love, and hope to those in need.

Learn more at:
- www.feeonlyretirement.com

CHAPTER 8

EVERYONE HAS A STORY THAT MATTERS

BY NICK NANTON, DNA MEDIA

It's my personal belief that God puts every single human being on this planet for a purpose. If we're willing to be vulnerable, most of us don't even know exactly what purpose we serve right now, and that's ok! In fact, sometimes it may take decades or even a lifetime to discover our unique purpose and how we can best serve the greater good. Sadly, some people never find out or realize how they best serve. But what we do know, if you share my sentiment from the first line above, is that we are here for some good reason.

Many people often find their purpose and a sense of fulfillment in their work, families, volunteer activities, and hobbies. While some people are destined to be presidents, political figures, international film stars, major sports figures, religious or spiritual leaders, others are destined to serve in simpler, quieter ways. Highly visible, public lives are not for everyone. But no matter what role you play, rest assured, your purpose is integral, and important, to more people than you may ever know.

Today, my life's mission and driving purpose (and yes, I spent a lot of time and had a lot of coaching and feedback to figure this out) is *to have meaningful conversations that lead to produced outcomes*. What that really boils down to is having great conversations with interesting people, and then we'll decide what we want to do together. Then, I bring in my team to help me accomplish it, so I can stay in my lane and continue to have meaningful conversations (while trying not to get bogged down in every step of the process it takes to produce something that we are all proud of). One of the outcomes I produce with my team happens to be documentaries. I love meeting people and helping them tell their stories in ways that touch the greatest number of people. The right story can change the way we view anything and everything. We just have to hear a story that we believe is authentically and honestly told. My favorite kind of stories are the ones that give us all hope.

STORIES IGNITED MY PASSION AND MISSION TO SHARE AND TO SERVE

I have been intrigued by stories since I was a kid. I started writing songs when I was fifteen. I especially loved stories that were told through songs. From my earliest memories, stories have piqued my curiosity, they have stimulated my imagination and have become the driving force of my life. The stories in which people overcame great odds, or went out of their way to help someone who was suffering, always made me want to be a better person by doing something to help and serve others.

Other people's stories also ignited a deep passion in me to share my story in any way that could also serve others. So many of the stories that have been shared with me over the years have had life-changing effects on me, as well as others I've been able to share those stories with—whether that is from sharing the story in person at a speaking engagement or through the medium of a documentary.

SHARE YOUR WISDOM

After speaking engagements, I am often asked by people in the audience how they might become a speaker or a coach or a 'whatever.' They invariably follow that question with a self-conscious statement of uneasiness, "I'd feel like an imposter." or "I'm not sure that I have anything to share." Many times this comes from having been trained to have a victim mentality. I am not saying some people aren't victims of terrible circumstances...but the people I generally can help would more identify as survivors, rather than victims. The Victim Mentality is a syndrome that runs deep throughout our society. That's why so few people step out and break through their fears and insecurities to discover that their dream (of becoming a coach, speaker, writer, or whatever it is they long to be or accomplish) is not as difficult as they imagined.

Going back to the God-given purpose behind the existence of every human being, if you have a burning desire to do anything, consider the fact that this desire is your inner purpose urging you on...urging you to go for it. It doesn't matter how 'profound'you think your topic is...or isn't. *If it is important to you, it will be important to someone else.*

My own story is deeply intertwined with the people I meet, especially those who ask for help or guidance when they want to accomplish something they feel inspired to do. I encourage them not to overthink things. For those who believe they have nothing to say, I tell them you never know whose life you may touch or even change, by stepping out and making your own dream a reality.

I especially love hearing stories of people older than I am. For instance, think about this. If you're 40 and the person who is sharing their wisdom is 80 years old, you could think of it as getting a 40-year shortcut. And even if you are younger than the person you are sharing your story with, you have lived a different life than they have, so by finding and sharing your individual and unique brand of wisdom, you could be saving them from 40 years of trying to figure out something too! Think of it as your obligation to share what you know, with those that you care about. You've got to stop worrying about the value you personally put on what you know. It's common human behavior! What we don't know, we put a huge premium on, because we don't know it! But what we do know, we assume everyone must know!

When you feel driven to share your story, you don't know who you will be helping. That part doesn't matter. In fact, let's say you decided to write a book, or a chapter in a book like this one. You could be long gone, and someone could come across the book and your story could completely change their lives. We don't always understand God's plan. But our purpose is embedded in our individual DNA. Can't you feel it? Haven't you thought or maybe even said it out loud, "I know I was created for more than this?"

We all know a lot about what we know. So, with a little self-searching, if you are called to serve through speaking, writing, coaching, or sharing in any way, you will simply need to find that seed of authenticity that will help your mission blossom and flower. These seeds will draw your audience to you. As so many have done before, you can do this too.

STARTING IS ALWAYS THE HARDEST PART

Most of the people I meet who are looking for guidance don't quite know where to begin. When you have an urgent calling, you can't pass it by. In other words, your drive will be so overwhelming that you will find a way to accomplish it, and nothing will ever get in the way to stop you. For others who aren't quite as confident, the way forward might not be as clear. One story I love to share with people who are seeking their purpose is a tidbit I learned from a man who wanted to become a champion poker player, and did accomplish his goal. I asked him what he considered to be the number one skill one must have to be a champion poker player. Without hesitation, he said, 'Self-awareness.' I would argue that holds true for any endeavor in life. Cultivate self-awareness first. That one skill will help you in any other endeavor that calls to you. It has certainly been an important skill that I continue to develop.

HOW TO DISCOVER YOUR AUTHENTICITY AND GROW A FOLLOWING

Starting is the hardest part of any journey. However, I have a simple method that I share which is helpful for exploring and getting started on your search for your seed idea that can give life and authenticity to your story. In fact, it may inspire you to go even further. First, sit down in front of your computer, or better yet, with a blank sheet of paper. You're going to make three lists.

Each list will represent a seminal period of your life. It should be any period that was of great meaning to you. Then, for each list, write down your top five most positive experiences during each of those three timeframes. Follow that with the five most negative experiences that occurred during the same three timeframes.

Everything you write down was part of your experience...what created you...what helped you arrive where you are right now. And everything you write down, by the mere fact you remembered it as a part of conducting this exercise, is important to who you are right now at this moment in your life!

Once you have your lists completed, write down why these times were so powerful for you... write down what these times meant to you. These are the moments that made you who you are. They are where you came from. And they will likely be able to point you in the direction where you are now meant to go.

Depending on how you want to share your story, you'll want to consider the medium for getting your story out there. Do you want to write a book? Do you want to tell your story to live audiences a la TED Talks or perhaps in other local venues? Do you want to share your story strictly via an online presence? Do you want to be a life coach or a business coach? Do you want to have a podcast? You will want to decide on a vehicle that you're comfortable with, as not everyone is comfortable in front of a camera or on a stage. This is an important part of the decision-making process before you can move forward.

MANAGE EXPECTATIONS

Once you can see your direction and the excitement builds, here's something else to remember as you continue forward: Not everything catches on like wildfire. You must have patience and perseverance in developing your idea(s), and while waiting to see results. In other words, you must manage your expectations. To do that, you must know what your expectations are. It's like any seed that you plant in the ground. You don't expect to see the seedling pop its head through the soil immediately, nor do you expect to harvest the fruit of that seed a week or two after you planted it. One of my mentors, Dr. Nido Qubein, is well known for saying "there is no such thing as an unrealistic dream…just an unrealistic timeline."

NO ONE IS GOOD AT EVERYTHING, BUT EVERYONE IS GOOD AT SOMETHING

We live in a culture that expects everyone to be good at everything. But that's simply not possible, so give yourself a break. Maybe you'll need to re-examine what you think you want to do and make sure it aligns with your values. If you do the simple exercise I outlined earlier, you'll know whether you are chasing an impossible dream. By that I mean if you want to be a star NBA player, but you're 5ft. 4in. tall and have never picked up a basketball, it's likely not going to happen (this is part of that self-awareness we discussed earlier). So, to set out on that path may be ill-advised unless you have some natural ability to leap five feet off the ground. In that case, go for it!

I'm not suggesting that if something seems out of reach or difficult that it isn't achievable. I'm stating that each of us is already good at something, we don't have to be good at everything. Some things come easier than others. If what you want to do is something you love and something you realize for the first time that you are good at, then keep going.

Next, ask yourself if you want 'hobby' results or 'professional' results. My good friend, the renowned Strategic Coach founder, Dan Sullivan, suggests exploring and answering the question, "What would success look like to you?" Think about how much effort you want to put toward achieving your goal. And think about whether you want to make an income or a living from it. Sharing your story doesn't always have to result in monetization, but if it does, all the better.

YOUR STORY COULD INSPIRE HOPE OR EVEN SAVE SOMEONE'S LIFE

We all have stories that matter. Some people keep theirs bottled up until they are on their deathbed. I urge you to discover your authentic way of sharing your story before it's too late, because you simply never know who is waiting to be healed, helped, or inspired.

Today, with the internet, it's easy to share information. It's extraordinary how you can now find out how to do absolutely anything. People share their knowledge about what might seem to be the most insignificant things. I learned how to light a Big Green Egg charcoal grill on the internet. I had never done it before, so I looked up how to do it the right way! I have to say I am grateful for every bit of valuable information I find on the web. I've heard so many stories from friends about how they have learned some of the most basic formative skills just because someone had the urge to share their knowledge on the internet.

If you are not called to serve in a way that touches the lives of large numbers of people, don't worry. Maybe you are called to serve and share in smaller and less public ways. Perhaps you smile at the cashier in the supermarket every time you go through the line and that brightens his or her day. Maybe you serve by maintaining a calm presence in your workplace that positively affects your colleagues. Serving and sharing our gifts is individual and unique. However, if you are called into service in a more public way that reaches a multitude of people, then I say don't delay and definitely don't overthink it.

ONE INFLUENTIAL STORY THAT CHANGED MY LIFE

You may not be a sports fan, but even if you're not, you may have heard of legendary basketball commentator Dick Vitale – aka Dickie V.

Dickie V started out coaching middle school and high school sports teams. He then went on to coach college basketball where he came to notoriety for his vivacious, colorful personality and his ability to win against all odds. He then went on to coach the pros. He went from high school sidelines to coaching in the NBA in just seven short years! That's quite a meteoric rise. I was fortunate enough to direct and produce a documentary on this legendary coach. As a casual basketball fan, I was aware of Dickie V and his legendary personality and ability to lead a team to victory—but there was so much more to the story that myself and millions of people worldwide didn't know.

What I learned from Dickie V's story is that what one does as a 'career' is merely the backdrop to whom a person really is. Everyone's life is filled with ups and downs, heartaches and heartbreaks, successes and failures. But it's how one reacts in the face of what life throws at you that speaks to your true character. What I learned from working with Dickie V and getting to know him is that tenacity, that sense of never giving up, is one trait that people with a burning desire, a passion and a mission have in common. This experience taught me that fortune really does favor the bold.

I love people and helping people. I love learning interesting things and meeting interesting people. My life's mission and passion has become crystal clear in my role as a film director. It is to have the most meaningful conversations that hopefully help somebody. If I can help someone by telling my story and/ or by helping someone tell their story, I am fulfilled. Everyone has a story that matters. I hope you find yours and share it with the world.

About Nick

From the slums of Port au Prince, Haiti, with special forces raiding a sex-trafficking ring and freeing children, to the Virgin Galactic Space Port in Mojave with Sir Richard Branson, the 22-Time Emmy Award Winning Director/Producer, Nick Nanton, has become known for telling stories that connect. Why? Because he focuses on the most fascinating subject in the world: PEOPLE. As a storyteller and Best-Selling Author, Nick has shared his message with millions of people through his documentaries, speeches, blogs, lectures, and best-selling books. Nick's book *StorySelling* hit *The Wall Street Journal* Best-Seller list and is available on Audible as an audio book. Nick has directed more than 60 documentaries and a sold out Broadway Show (garnering 43 Emmy nominations in multiple regions and 22 wins), including:

- DREAM BIG: Rudy Ruettiger LIVE on Broadway
- Visioneer: The Peter Diamandis Story
- Rudy Ruettiger: The Walk On
- Operation Toussaint
- The Rebound

Nick has shared the stage, co-authored books, and made films featuring:

- – Larry King
- – Dick Vitale
- – Kenny Chesney
- – Charles Barkley
- – Coach Mike Krzyzewksi
- – Jack Nicklaus
- – Tony Robbins
- – Steve Forbes
- – will.i.am
- – Sir Richard Branson
- – Dean Kamen
- – Ray Kurzweil
- – Lisa Nichols
- – Peter Diamandis
  ......and many more

Nick specializes in bringing the element of human connection to every viewer, no matter the subject. He is currently directing and hosting the series *In Case You Didn't Know* (Season 1 Executive Produced by Larry King), featuring legends in the worlds of business, entrepreneurship, personal development, technology, and sports.